STAR WARS™

CODING PROJECTS

DK | Penguin Random House

Senior Editor Elizabeth Dowsett
Senior Designers Owen Bennett and Clive Savage
Pre-production Producer Rebecca Fallowfield
Producer Zara Markland
Managing Editor Sadie Smith
Managing Art Editor Ron Stobbart
Publisher Julie Ferris
Art Director Lisa Lanzarini
Publishing Director Simon Beecroft

First published in Great Britain in 2017 by
Dorling Kindersley Limited
80 Strand, London WC2R 0RL
A Penguin Random House Company

10 9 8 7 6 5 4 3 2 1
001–306471–October/17

A CIP catalogue record for this book
is available from the British Library.

ISBN: 978-0-24130-578-2

Printed in China.

A WORLD OF IDEAS:
SEE ALL THERE IS TO KNOW

www.dk.com
www.starwars.com

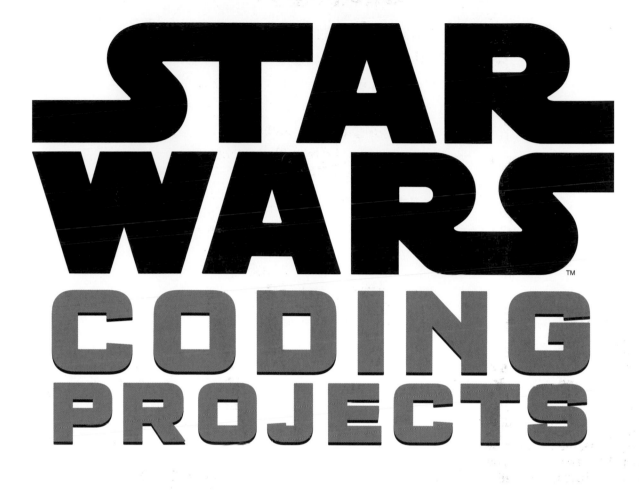

STAR WARS™
CODING PROJECTS

WRITTEN BY **JON WOODCOCK**
ILLUSTRATED BY **JON HALL**

Contents

You can dip in and out of this book and make whichever games you like. However, if you're new to Scratch, it's best to work through the games in the order they appear. This will help you build a good understanding of how Scratch works.

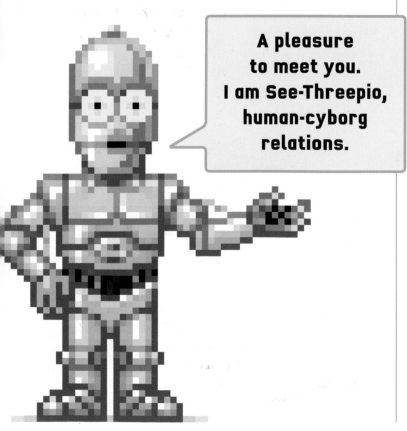

A pleasure to meet you. I am See-Threepio, human-cyborg relations.

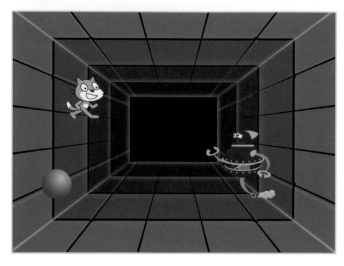

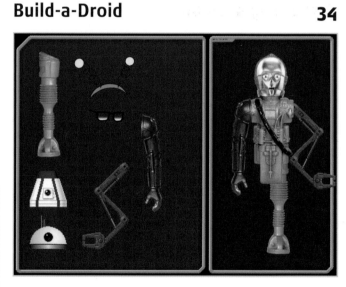

Use the Force!

Secret Spy Mission

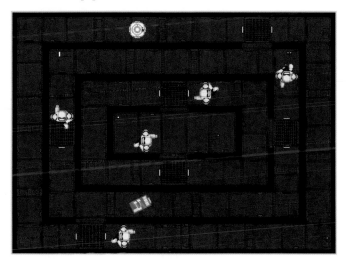

Asteroid Dash

Glossary
How to Get Scratch

Just the beginning, this is.

How to use this book

Scratch is about inventing, experimenting and having fun. The projects in this book use *Star Wars* themes, but you can draw your own pictures and record your own sounds. There are also plenty of ready-made images and sounds in the Scratch libraries loaded and waiting for you to use and even customise.

To learn how to draw your own sprites, see pages 14 and 15.

Use your imagination to bring your own ideas to life, just like Anakin Skywalker did. He used spare parts to build his own droid − called C-3PO!

Foreword

Growing up in a world where computers are part of everything from spaceships to microwaves, we can be sure that technology is here to stay! If you know how to use computers, the universe opens up and shows you everything that is possible. When you learn how to *program* computers, you can make the impossible feel real, too. Nobody knows this better than the creative teams behind the *Star Wars* movies.

Even back in 1977, before tablets and smartphones, *Star Wars* showcased detailed animation programs written by an extremely intelligent computer artist named Larry Cuba. His passion and imagination helped to launch an industry that has caused generations of moviegoers to believe in a freighter ship with three droid brains and holoprojectors that recreate galaxies in the palm of your hand.

Today, more than 40 years later, technology has come so far that kids just like you can easily create programs to keep yourselves entertained, help make difficult decisions or solve problems. Surprisingly, the skills to create this kind of life-altering software don't have to begin in the classroom. These skills start with a passion for experimentation and a willingness to make mistakes.

Like exploring the galaxy, programming is a learning experience.

THE BEST DISCOVERIES HAPPEN WHEN YOU ARE CONFIDENT ENOUGH IN YOURSELF TO WALK INTO THE UNKNOWN AND TAKE A LOOK AROUND.

Make a move. See what happens. You don't need to know everything about your environment before you start building something new. If your creation fails, learn from your mistakes and keep going. Be as proud of the problems that you work hard to solve as you are of a program that has no errors at all.

With this book, you carry with you a guide to one of the world's most beloved block-based programming languages: Scratch. Scratch was developed as a way of allowing people to express themselves through stories and games, using simple, puzzle-like code. Although Scratch was created for children aged eight and up, it was later adopted in college classrooms as a way of teaching the basics of computer science without the worry of having to learn a complicated programming environment. Now, *you* get to benefit from this simple-to-use software, as you drop yourself into the many exciting worlds of *Star Wars*.

With detailed and easy-to-follow lessons by Jon Woodcock, *Star Wars Coding Projects* will help you learn basic coding concepts as you dive into fun and playful programs.

YOU MIGHT FEEL LIKE YOU'RE PLAYING A GAME, BUT IN REALITY, YOU'RE DEVELOPING A NEW WAY OF THINKING AND PROBLEM-SOLVING THAT WILL CHANGE THE WAY YOU LOOK AT THE WORLD.

If you remember to keep an open mind and celebrate both your successes *and* failures, you just might find that a few hours of coding turns into a lifetime of changing what is possible.

KIKI PROTTSMAN
Curriculum Development Manager at Code.org
Author and YouTube Personality for KIKIvsIT

The Force is calling to you. Just let it in.

Computer Coding

In the galaxy far, far away, computers are everywhere: in droids, comlinks, datapads, weapons and vehicles. In our galaxy, too, computers are all around us: A smartphone is a computer that fits in your pocket. Cars, just like starfighters, contain dozens of computers. But how do these computers know what to do? It's all thanks to coding.

X-wings have many computers working their different parts.

What is coding?

Coding, or computer programming, is telling a computer what to do. In this book you'll learn how to control a computer, like Obi-Wan Kenobi controls a stormtrooper on Tatooine with a Jedi mind trick. Computers need detailed instructions. They must be broken down into simple steps that the computer can follow in order. These steps make up what is called an "algorithm".

What are computer languages?

For a computer to follow the steps of an algorithm, they must be written in a special "programming language" that the computer can understand. There are many programming languages. Some have strange names like C#, C++, Python and Java, which would suit *Star Wars* droids and characters. In this book you'll learn how to make programs in Scratch, which is a simple programming language for beginners.

I am fluent in over seven million forms of communication.

Code words

Algorithm A set of instructions that are followed in order to perform a particular task. Computer programs are based on algorithms.

Bug A mistake in a program.

Code Computer instructions written in a programming language are often called code. Coding is programming.

Debugging Finding and removing bugs from pieces of code.

Program Instructions written in a programming language that a computer can follow.

Run The command to tell a computer to carry out the instructions in a program.

Trash compactor algorithm

The computer controlling the Death Star trash compactor probably had quite a simple algorithm. After all, it only needed to squash rubbish. It probably looked something like this:

> ➤ Wait 12 hours.

> ➤ Move walls in 5 m (16 ft) to crush the rubbish.

> ➤ Dump the crushed rubbish.

> ➤ Move walls back to starting position.

> ➤ Go back to the start.

Deep in the Death Star, Princess Leia, Luke Skywalker, Han Solo and Chewbacca found themselves trapped in a room of rubbish. Then the walls started moving in.

R2-D2 quickly got to work, accessing the Death Star's computer systems with a special arm attachment to rewrite the programming.

When R2-D2's friends were stuck in the trash compactor, the droid had to connect to the Death Star's computer to stop them from getting crushed. He probably made changes like this:

> ➤ Wait 12 hours.

> ➤ Move walls in 2 m (6 ft) to crush the garbage.

⋮...... Reducing the distance the walls moved would stop R2-D2's friends from being crushed.

> ➤ Wait 10 minutes.

⋮...... Inserting a delay here would give his friends time to escape.

> ➤ Move walls in 3 m (10 ft).

Moving the walls 3 m (10 ft) more here brings the walls completely together.

> ➤ Dump the crushed rubbish.

> ➤ Move walls back to starting position.

> ➤ Go back to the start.

What is Scratch?

Scratch is a programming language designed for beginners. It uses simple, ready-made blocks to build programs. Getting started in Scratch is really easy, and the sky's the limit when it comes to what you can create.

What's what in Scratch?

In Scratch projects, programs called "scripts" control characters and objects known as "sprites". The sprites appear in a part of the Scratch screen called the "STAGE".

Sprites

Sprites are objects that move around on the STAGE in a project. They may be animals, Jedi, lightsabers or spaceships. Scripts bring sprites to life.

This cat sprite appears whenever you start a new project. Scratch Cat is the symbol of Scratch.

Scripts

Scripts are made of coloured blocks that you drag with a computer mouse and put together like jigsaw puzzle pieces. Each block contains one instruction. Scratch reads through a script from top to bottom.

```
when        clicked
move  10  steps
say  Roger, roger!
```

.... Script makes battle droid sprite walk 10 steps, then say "Roger, roger!"

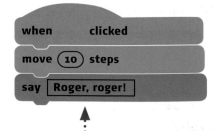

Roger, roger!

Blocks for everything

Scratch has instruction blocks that can do many different things. Here's a tiny selection:

```
wait  2  secs
```
.... Wait a moment

```
go to  mouse-pointer ▼
```
Move a sprite ....

```
7 + 22
```
.... Do maths

```
change  color ▼  effect by  -5
```
Change a colour ....

```
play note  60 ▼  for  0.5  beats
```
.... Make some music

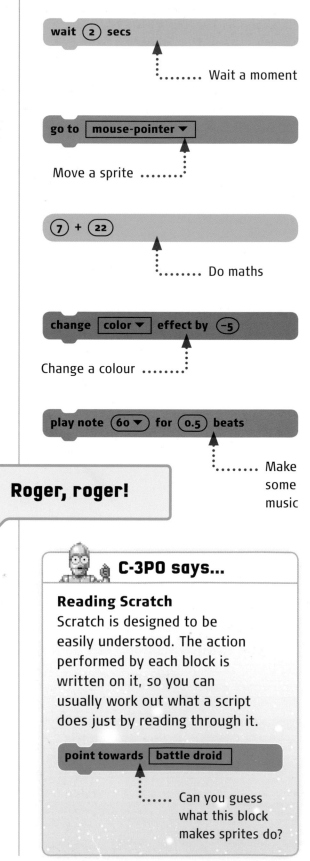

C-3PO says...

Reading Scratch
Scratch is designed to be easily understood. The action performed by each block is written on it, so you can usually work out what a script does just by reading through it.

```
point towards  battle droid
```
.... Can you guess what this block makes sprites do?

The STAGE

The action in a Scratch project, such as Jetpack Adventure (see pages 48 to 59), takes place on the STAGE. Sprites can move around the STAGE, in front of a background image called a "backdrop". Scratch measures distances on the STAGE in units called "steps". The STAGE is 480 steps wide and 360 steps tall.

The green flag starts, or runs, the project. This activates all the scripts that you've built.

The red button stops all scripts.

The character, the fuel canister and the electrified barrier are all sprites.

STAGE

Each sprite is controlled by its own scripts, which tell it how to move, change size and more.

Backdrop helps create atmosphere.

Jetpack Adventure
Ruthless Bounty Hunter

I want to learn the ways of the Force.

Projects, projects, projects

Scratch has endless possibilities and is all about experimenting. In the Explore section of the Scratch website, you'll see millions of projects (yes, millions!) made by people just like you. You can make stories, animations, games, music, art. Let your imagination run wild!

Scratch 2.0

This book is based on Scratch 2.0 — the latest version of Scratch at the time of writing. The projects won't work on older versions, so make sure you have 2.0. See page 96 for details on how to get Scratch.

Exploring Scratch

When you launch the Scratch editor, this is what you will see. The tools for building scripts are on the right, while the STAGE to the left shows you what's going on as your project runs. Don't be afraid to explore!

Change language

Menus

Cursor tools

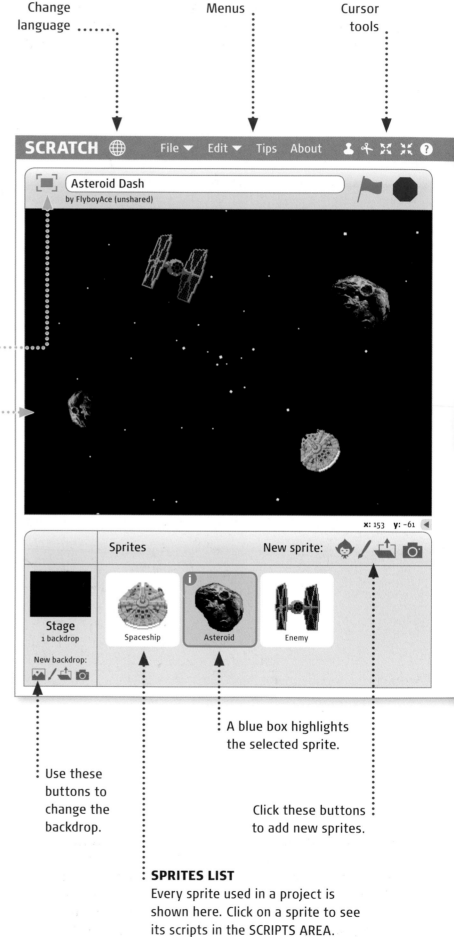

Click here for a full-screen view of your project.

STAGE
This is where the action happens. When you run your project, the STAGE is where all the sprites appear, moving and interacting as they follow their scripts.

Naming the parts

While using this book, you'll need to know what's where in the Scratch window. Shown here are the names of the different areas. The tabs at the top of the BLOCKS PALETTE open up other areas of Scratch to edit sounds and sprite costumes.

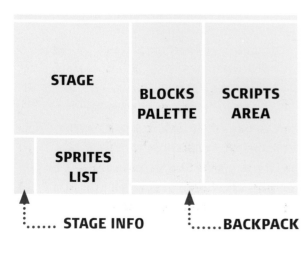

Use these buttons to change the backdrop.

A blue box highlights the selected sprite.

Click these buttons to add new sprites.

SPRITES LIST
Every sprite used in a project is shown here. Click on a sprite to see its scripts in the SCRIPTS AREA.

Select the SCRIPTS tab to build scripts.

Use the COSTUMES tab to change how sprites look.

Use the SOUNDS tab to add music and sound effects to sprites.

SCRIPTS AREA
Drag blocks into this part of the Scratch window and join them together to build scripts for each sprite in your project.

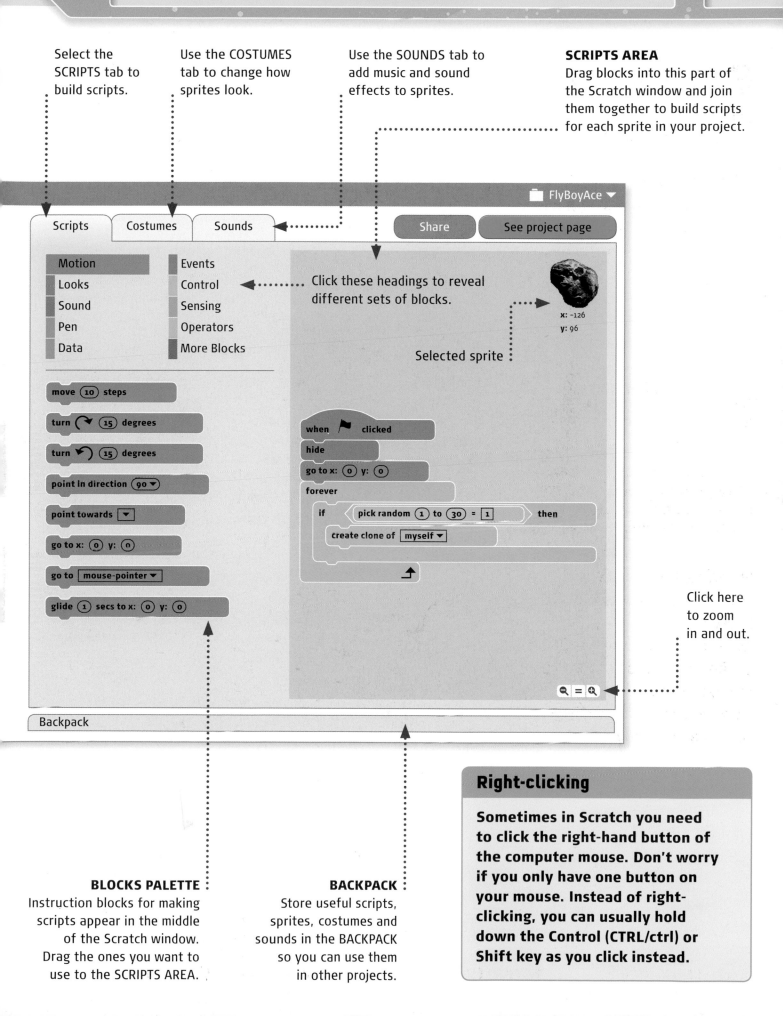

FlyBoyAce ▾

Scripts Costumes Sounds

Share   See project page

Motion
Looks
Sound
Pen
Data

Events
Control
Sensing
Operators
More Blocks

Click these headings to reveal different sets of blocks.

x: –126
y: 96

Selected sprite

move (10) steps

turn ↻ (15) degrees

turn ↺ (15) degrees

point in direction (90 ▾)

point towards [▾]

go to x: (0) y: (0)

go to [mouse-pointer ▾]

glide (1) secs to x: (0) y: (0)

when ⚑ clicked
hide
go to x: (0) y: (0)
forever
  if ⟨ pick random (1) to (30) = [1] ⟩ then
    create clone of [myself ▾]

Click here to zoom in and out.

⊖ = ⊕

Backpack

BLOCKS PALETTE
Instruction blocks for making scripts appear in the middle of the Scratch window. Drag the ones you want to use to the SCRIPTS AREA.

BACKPACK
Store useful scripts, sprites, costumes and sounds in the BACKPACK so you can use them in other projects.

Right-clicking

Sometimes in Scratch you need to click the right-hand button of the computer mouse. Don't worry if you only have one button on your mouse. Instead of right-clicking, you can usually hold down the Control (CTRL/ctrl) or Shift key as you click instead.

DATABANK

Using Images in Scratch

To create projects in Scratch, you need images. Each sprite needs an image and you can also decorate the STAGE with a backdrop image behind the action. There are four ways to get images for your projects. For more detailed information on these, see pages 36 to 42.

Four ways to make sprites

New sprite: 👤 / 📤 📷

The NEW SPRITE menu is found just below the STAGE.

1 Use the Scratch image library

To choose a ready-to-use sprite from the Scratch sprite library, click the sprite library button [👤] in the NEW SPRITE menu. If the image isn't exactly what you want, you can customise it using the built-in paint editor.

2 Draw your own image

The possibilities are endless if you draw your own sprite using Scratch's built-in paint editor software. To draw an image, click on the paintbrush icon [/] in the NEW SPRITE menu.

3 Upload your own photo

To use an image stored on your computer, click the file icon [📤] in the NEW SPRITE menu and select the photo you want to use. If you don't want the whole image, you can cut out an area of it using the paint editor.

4 Use a webcam

Click on the camera icon [📷] in the NEW SPRITE menu to use your webcam to take a photo to use in Scratch. If you don't want to use the whole image, the paint editor allows you to cut out the area you want.

You need a teacher. I can show you the ways of the Force.

Backdrop images

The background of your game can be decorated with a picture, too. Backdrop images work exactly the same way as sprite images. The icons are the same, except for the backdrop library button [🖼]. They are all found in the NEW BACKDROP menu.

Stage
1 backdrop

New backdrop:
🖼 / 📤 📷

Click here to access the library of backdrop images.

The paint editor

You can draw anything with Scratch's built-in paint editor. Once you've made your sprite, look carefully around your drawing for unwanted pixels and erase them as they may stop the game from working correctly. You'll also need to centre your sprite (see below).

C-3PO says...

Pixels

A pixel (short for "picture element") is the smallest dot of colour that can be shown on screen. It's the size of the tiniest Scratch paintbrush speck.

Undo takes you back in time. This is useful if you make a mistake.

Redo

Crop

Flip tools

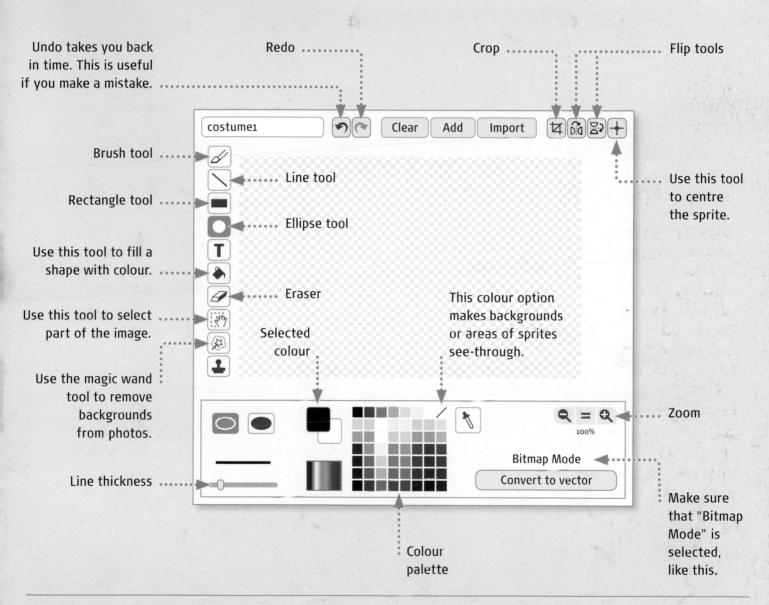

Brush tool

Line tool

Rectangle tool

Ellipse tool

Use this tool to fill a shape with colour.

Eraser

This colour option makes backgrounds or areas of sprites see-through.

Use this tool to select part of the image.

Selected colour

Use the magic wand tool to remove backgrounds from photos.

Use this tool to centre the sprite.

Line thickness

Zoom

Bitmap Mode

Colour palette

Make sure that "Bitmap Mode" is selected, like this.

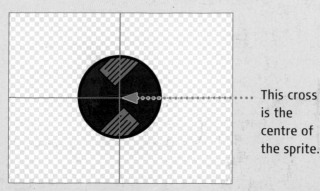

This cross is the centre of the sprite.

Centring sprites

If you draw your own sprite in the paint editor, you'll need to tell Scratch where its centre is so that it can be placed in the correct position on the STAGE. Select the set costume centre tool [+], found in the top-right corner. A cross will appear over your image. Drag it to the centre of your sprite. Now your sprite is centred and ready to be used in a project.

DATABANK

Using Sound in Scratch

Sound adds atmosphere to games and projects in Scratch, whether it's a one-off noise when something happens or constant background music. There are three ways to add sounds to play in your projects, all found under the SOUNDS tab at the top of the Scratch editor.

Three ways to get sound

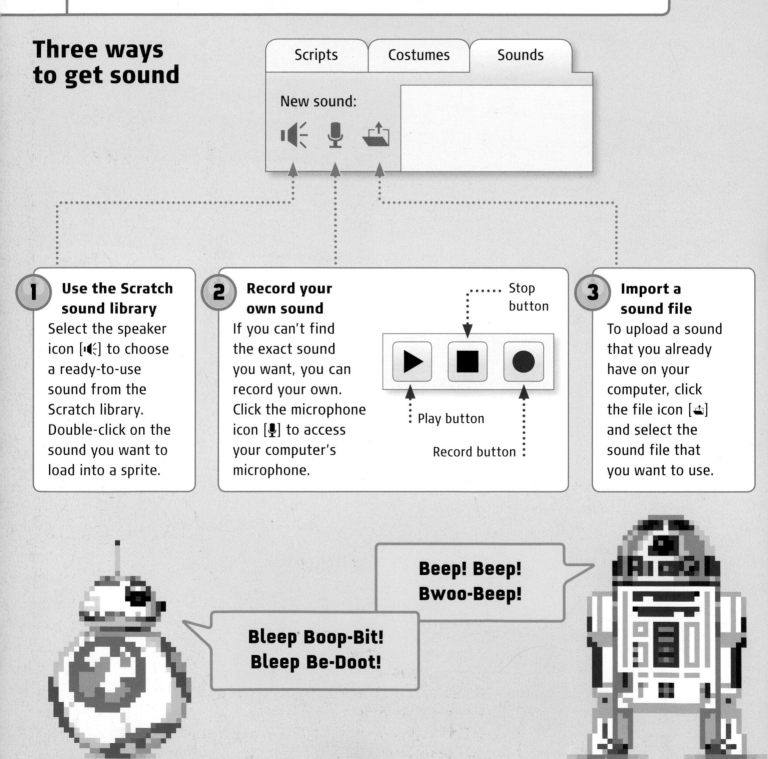

Scripts | Costumes | Sounds

New sound:

1 **Use the Scratch sound library**
Select the speaker icon [🔊] to choose a ready-to-use sound from the Scratch library. Double-click on the sound you want to load into a sprite.

2 **Record your own sound**
If you can't find the exact sound you want, you can record your own. Click the microphone icon [🎤] to access your computer's microphone.

Stop button

Play button

Record button

3 **Import a sound file**
To upload a sound that you already have on your computer, click the file icon [⬆] and select the sound file that you want to use.

Beep! Beep! Bwoo-Beep!

Bleep Boop-Bit! Bleep Be-Doot!

The sound editor

Once you've loaded a sound into a sprite, it will appear as a trace in the sound editor. You can use the editor to get rid of unwanted parts or add effects.

You can always click the undo button if things go wrong, so don't be afraid to experiment!

The tallest parts are the loudest.

Click and drag the mouse to select part of the recording to delete, copy or add an effect.

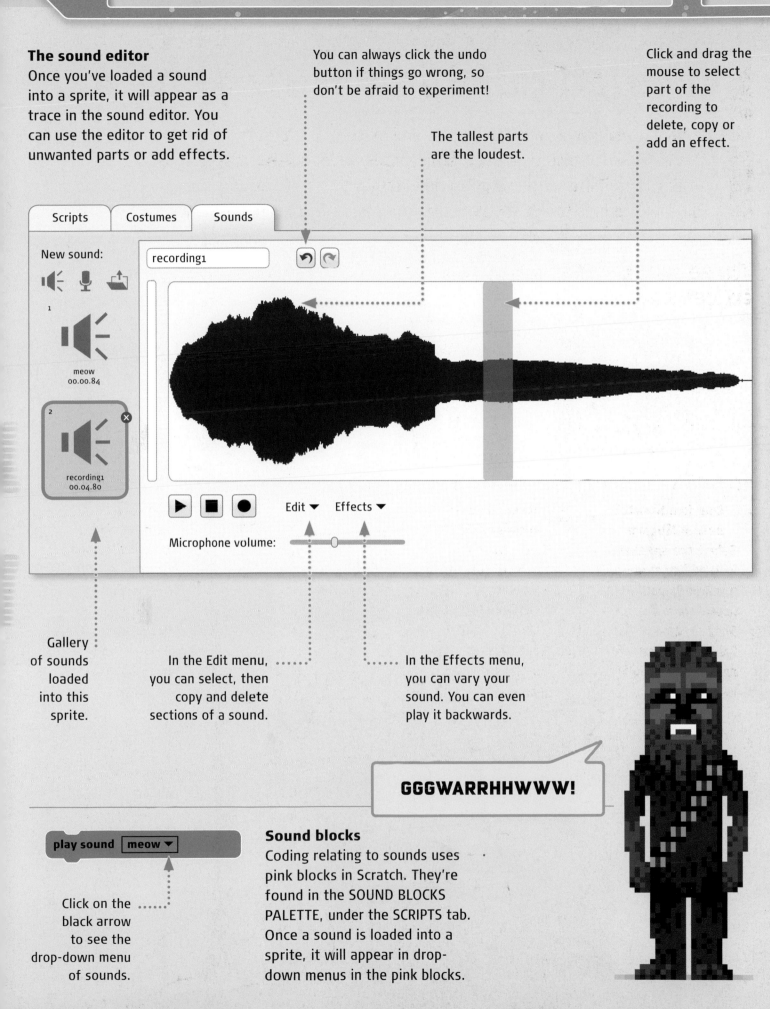

| Scripts | Costumes | Sounds |

New sound:

1

meow
00.00.84

2

recording1
00.04.80

recording1

Microphone volume:

Edit ▼   Effects ▼

Gallery of sounds loaded into this sprite.

In the Edit menu, you can select, then copy and delete sections of a sound.

In the Effects menu, you can vary your sound. You can even play it backwards.

GGGWARRHHWWW!

play sound meow ▼

Click on the black arrow to see the drop-down menu of sounds.

Sound blocks

Coding relating to sounds uses pink blocks in Scratch. They're found in the SOUND BLOCKS PALETTE, under the SCRIPTS tab. Once a sound is loaded into a sprite, it will appear in drop-down menus in the pink blocks.

Cargo Bay Chase

Calling all Scratch Padawans! Start your Scratch journey with this fun game of quick reactions. It uses Scratch's built-in art and sounds to help you understand the basics of script building. Once you've made the game, you can customise it to give it your own style.

Aim of the game

Scratch Cat needs to collect the bouncing energy balls without touching the evil robot. You move the cat around the STAGE using the mouse-pointer. Each ball you collect scores you a point. The evil robot is also chasing the energy balls. You'll need your wits about you, because the robot gets quicker with each ball it collects!

> I can assure you, they will never get me onto one of those dreadful starships!

This window displays your score. The more balls you collect, the higher your score.

Cargo Bay Chase
by ScruffyLookingNerfHerder (unshared)

CatScore   6

You control Scratch Cat with the mouse.

The cat collects energy balls by touching them.

The game's action takes place inside the cargo bay of a starship.

Click on the green flag to start the game.

Click on the red button to stop everything.

How to build the game

The first step is to make the Cat sprite follow the mouse-pointer around the STAGE. To do this, you need to build a set of instructions called a "script".

1 Start a new project. If you use Scratch online, go to the Scratch website and click on "Create" at the top. If you use Scratch offline, click on the Scratch desktop icon. A fresh project will open, ready for you to start building scripts.

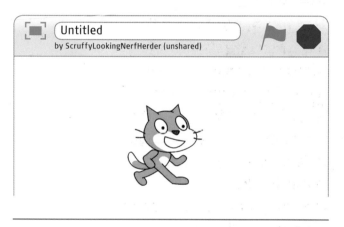

2 You build scripts by dragging coloured blocks from the middle area (the BLOCKS PALETTE) to the empty grey space on the right (the SCRIPTS AREA). The blocks are colour-coded by what they do. You can switch between different sets of blocks by clicking on the categories at the top of the BLOCKS PALETTE.

Motion is always selected when you start a new project. Clicking on each word shows a different set of coloured instruction blocks.

The evil robot is deadly — touch it, and it's game over! As the robot collects energy balls, it speeds up.

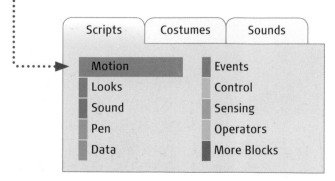

3 Click on the GO TO MOUSE-POINTER block and drag it into the SCRIPTS AREA on the right. It will stay where you put it.

go to | mouse-pointer ▼

Drag this block into the SCRIPTS AREA.

4 Now click on the CONTROL heading in the BLOCKS PALETTE. All the blocks in the centre of the Scratch window will switch to yellow.

| Scripts | Costumes | Sounds |

Motion   Events
Looks   Control
Sound   Sensing
Pen   Operators
Data   More Blocks

Click Control to reveal the yellow blocks.

wait (10) secs

repeat (10)

forever

Drag the FOREVER block to the SCRIPTS AREA.

5 Use the mouse to drag the FOREVER block around the GO TO MOUSE-POINTER block. It should click into place if you release it near the blue block. The FOREVER block makes the blocks inside run over and over again.

forever
  go to | mouse-pointer ▼

This block is called a "loop". It repeats any blocks you put inside it.

6 To complete your first script, select EVENTS heading in the BLOCKS PALETTE and then drag a WHEN ➤ CLICKED block to the top of your stack of blocks. This block makes the script run when someone clicks on the green flag [➤] at the top of the window.

This brown block runs the script.

when ⚑ clicked
forever
  go to | mouse-pointer ▼

7 To try out your script, click on the green flag [➤]. The cat will now go wherever the mouse-pointer goes on the STAGE. You can end the chase by clicking on the red stop button. Congratulations on completing your first working Scratch script!

Stops scripts ....
Starts scripts ....

Cargo Bay Chase   ⚑ ⬢
by ScruffyLookingNerfHerder (unshared)

C-3PO says...

Running programs
"Run a program" means "start a program" to a programmer. A program that's doing something is "running". In Scratch, programs are also called "projects", and clicking the green flag [➤] runs the current project and all the scripts within it.

8 The poor cat is just called "Sprite1", so rename it now. Select Sprite1 (the cat) in the SPRITES LIST and click on the blue "i" icon in the corner to get more information about the sprite. In the pop-up box, change the name to "Cat".

Type the sprite's new name here.

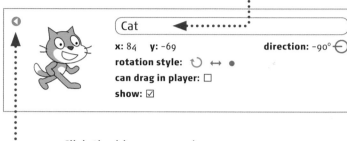

Cat

x: 84   y: -69   direction: -90°
rotation style: ↻ ↔ •
can drag in player: ☐
show: ☑

Click here to bring up the information pop-up box.

Click the blue arrow when you've remaned the cat to save this change.

The new name appears under the sprite.

Sprite1

Cat

Setting the scene

At the moment, the STAGE is just a boring white rectangle. You can create some atmosphere by adding a backdrop image as scenery.

9 To the left of the SPRITES LIST, in the NEW BACKDROP menu, is the icon for accessing the backdrop library []. Click on it and look for "neon tunnel". Select the image and click "OK". The backdrop will now fill the STAGE.

Type the name of your project here.

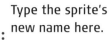

Click this icon to open the backdrop library.

Stage
1 backdrop

New backdrop:
🖼 ✏ ⬆ 📷

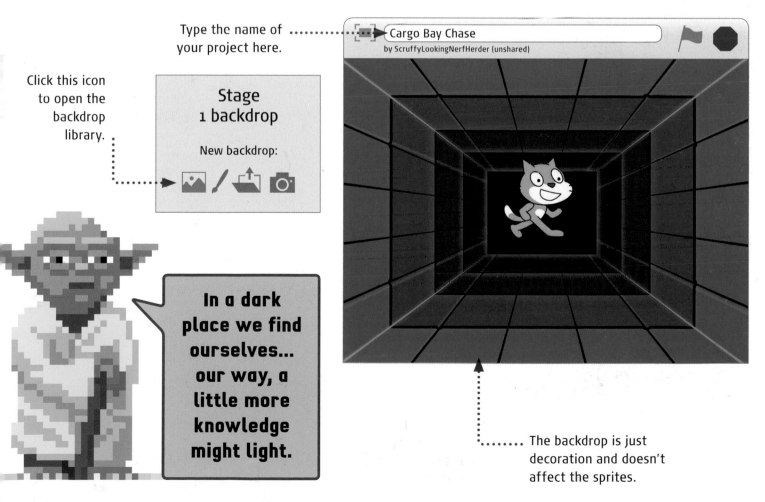

Cargo Bay Chase
by ScruffyLookingNerfHerder (unshared)

In a dark place we find ourselves... our way, a little more knowledge might light.

The backdrop is just decoration and doesn't affect the sprites.

Add the energy ball

Cats like to chase balls – and Scratch Cat is no exception! It's time to add a bouncing energy ball to the game. At first, the ball will just bounce back and forth across the STAGE, but later on you'll add the code to make it work in the game.

10 To add a second sprite to the project, click the "choose from the sprite library" button []. Select "Ball" and then click "OK".

Click here to open the sprite library.

The Ball sprite will appear in your SPRITES LIST.

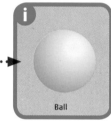

C-3PO says...

Loops

Most computer programs contain loops. These are useful, as they let a program go back and repeat a set of instructions, which keeps scripts simple and short. The FOREVER block creates a loop that goes on forever, but other loops can repeat an action a fixed number of times. You'll meet all sorts of clever loops in this book.

The script runs from top to bottom.

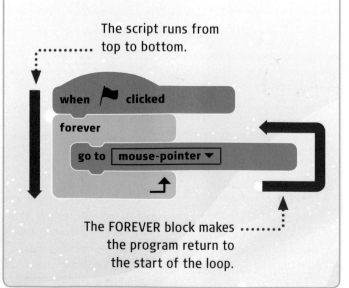

The FOREVER block makes the program return to the start of the loop.

11 Add the following script to the Ball sprite. To find the blue blocks, click on the MOTION BLOCKS PALETTE. The two dark-blue MOTION blocks used here make the ball move left and right across the STAGE.

This block runs the script when the game begins.

The FOREVER loop ensures that all the commands inside repeat.

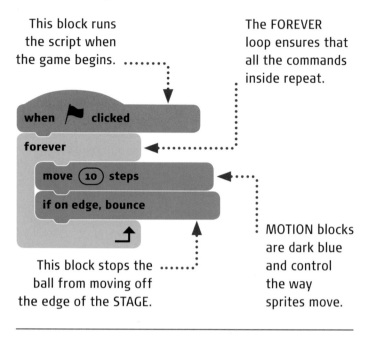

This block stops the ball from moving off the edge of the STAGE.

MOTION blocks are dark blue and control the way sprites move.

12 Click the green flag [] to run the project and watch the energy ball bounce back and forth across the STAGE. You can use the mouse to make the cat chase the ball, but nothing will happen yet if they touch.

The ball moves across the STAGE, bouncing off each edge.

Click the green flag to run the project.

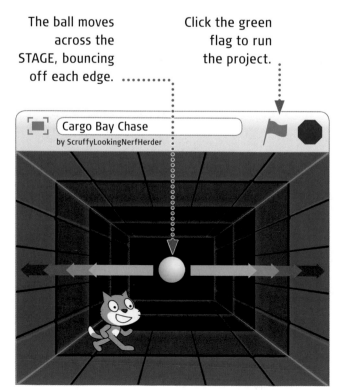

13 The energy balls aren't going to be much of a challenge to catch if they just move horizontally. Add a dark blue POINT IN DIRECTION block to the ball's script to change the direction it moves.

```
when 🏳 clicked
point in direction (45 ▼)
forever
    move (10) steps
    if on edge, bounce
```

Type 45 here to set the direction in which the ball moves.

 C-3PO says...

Directions

Scratch uses degrees (°) to set direction. You can choose any number from –179° to 180°. Negative numbers point sprites left; positive numbers point them right. Use 0° to go up and 180° to go straight down.

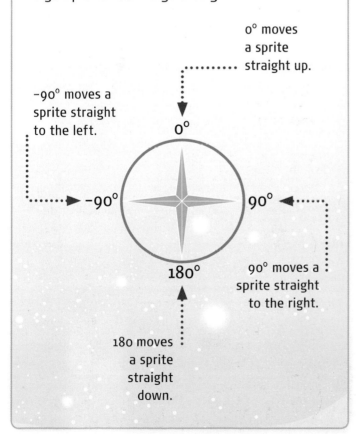

0° moves a sprite straight up.

–90° moves a sprite straight to the left.

0°

–90°

90°

180°

90° moves a sprite straight to the right.

180 moves a sprite straight down.

14 Click the green flag [🏳] to run the project and watch the ball move diagonally across the STAGE.

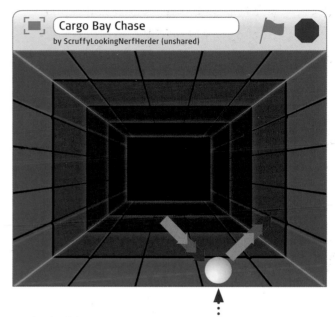

Cargo Bay Chase
by ScruffyLookingNerfHerder (unshared)

The ball bounces off the edges at an angle.

15 Experiment with the script by changing the number in the POINT IN DIRECTION block. Try numbers between –180 and 180. Run the project again for each number. Does the ball move off in the direction you expect it to?

Type your direction values in here.

```
when 🏳 clicked
point in direction (–30 ▼)
forever
    move (10) steps
    if on edge, bounce
```

Click on this triangle to see what happens.

16 Whatever value you use for the ball's direction, the ball will head off in that same direction each time you run the script. Click on the green OPERATORS blocks in the BLOCKS PALETTE. Drag a PICK RANDOM block into the window of the POINT IN DIRECTION block. Change the number range from 1 to 6 to –179 to 180.

The longing you seek is not behind you, it is in front of you.

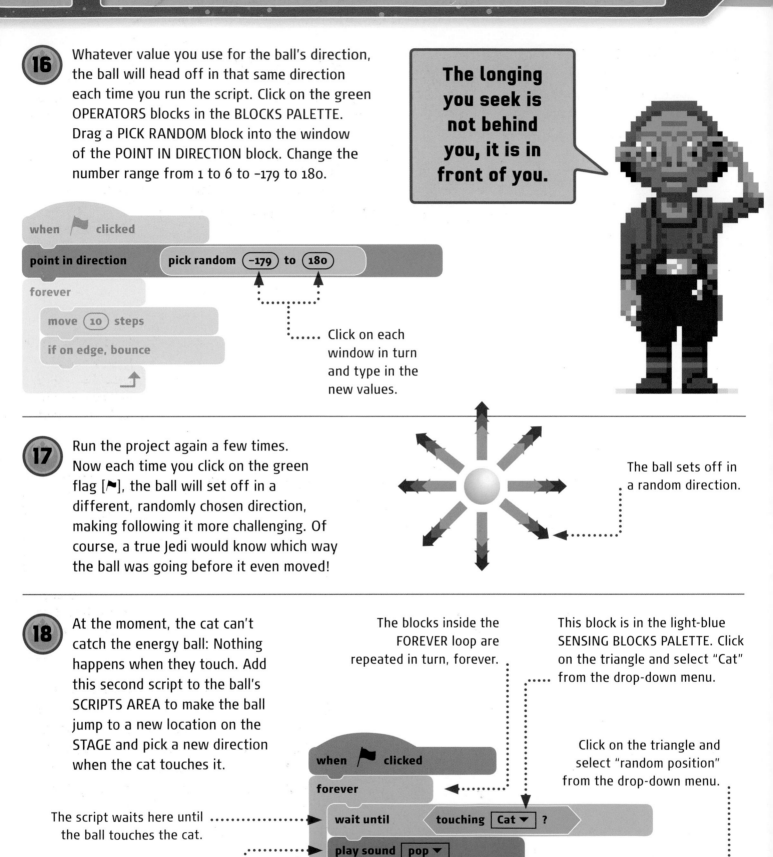

when ▶ clicked

point in direction   pick random (–179) to (180)

forever

move (10) steps

if on edge, bounce

Click on each window in turn and type in the new values.

17 Run the project again a few times. Now each time you click on the green flag [▶], the ball will set off in a different, randomly chosen direction, making following it more challenging. Of course, a true Jedi would know which way the ball was going before it even moved!

The ball sets off in a random direction.

18 At the moment, the cat can't catch the energy ball: Nothing happens when they touch. Add this second script to the ball's SCRIPTS AREA to make the ball jump to a new location on the STAGE and pick a new direction when the cat touches it.

The blocks inside the FOREVER loop are repeated in turn, forever.

This block is in the light-blue SENSING BLOCKS PALETTE. Click on the triangle and select "Cat" from the drop-down menu.

Click on the triangle and select "random position" from the drop-down menu.

when ▶ clicked

forever

The script waits here until the ball touches the cat.

wait until   touching Cat ▼ ?

You'll find this pink block in the SOUND BLOCKS PALETTE.

play sound pop ▼

go to random position ▼

point in direction   pick random (–179) to (180)

This block selects a new random direction for the ball.

19 Run the project. Both the ball's scripts will run at the same time. Use the mouse to make the cat touch the ball. The ball should jump to a new location on the STAGE and then move off in a new random direction.

When the cat and ball touch, the ball disappears with a pop and reappears in a new position.

Enter the evil robot

Every good game needs a baddie. This game has the evil robot, which tries to steal the energy balls before the cat gets them, increasing its power as it does so. Start by getting the robot to chase the energy ball.

20 In the NEW SPRITE menu, click on the "choose from the sprite library" button []. Select the sprite "Robot1", then click "OK".

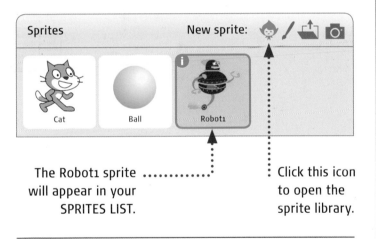

The Robot1 sprite will appear in your SPRITES LIST.

Click this icon to open the sprite library.

21 Make sure the Robot1 sprite is selected and appears with a blue frame around it in the SPRITES LIST. Then add this script to the robot's SCRIPTS AREA. The script tells the robot to turn towards the ball and then move forwards over and over.

You'll find this block in the purple LOOKS BLOCKS PALETTE. Type 50 in its window to shrink the robot.

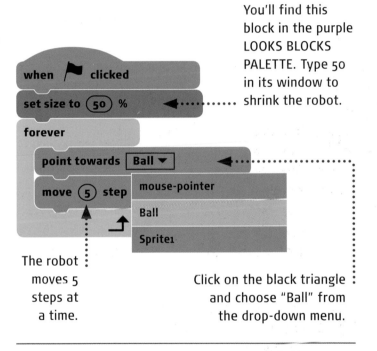

The robot moves 5 steps at a time.

Click on the black triangle and choose "Ball" from the drop-down menu.

22 Now run the script. The robot follows the ball, but it's upside down much of the time! To fix this, select the robot and click on the blue "i" icon. In the pop-up box, choose the middle of the three options after "rotation style". Now the robot will stay upright as it chases the ball round the STAGE.

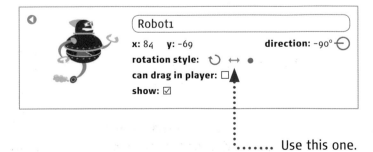

Use this one.

C-3PO says...

Random numbers

A random number is one that you can't predict before it appears. A dice roll gives a random number. Any number from one to six could appear, but you don't know which it will be until you roll. In Scratch, you can get a random number using the green PICK RANDOM block.

Lowest number it can select ....

Highest number ...... it can select

Make the robot deadly!

At the moment, Scratch Cat just ignores the robot. Add some code to fix this problem. It will stop the game when the cat detects that it's touching the robot. Run away, Scratch Cat!

This will shrink the cat to match the size of the robot.

Add this IF-THEN block with the other blocks inside it. They are only run if the cat touches the robot.

This block stops every script in the project, ending the game.

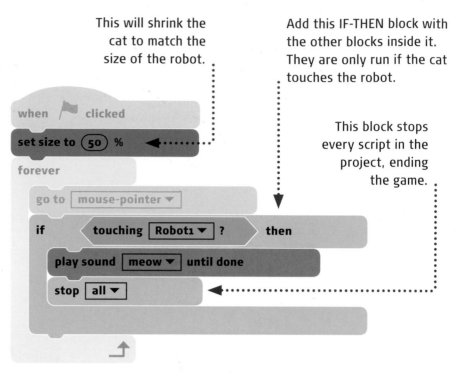

 23 Select the Cat sprite in the SPRITES LIST and change its script as shown on the right. Read the script – what do you think it does? The blocks inside the IF-THEN block run only if the cat touches the robot. It's a good idea to shrink the cat to match the robot with a new SET SIZE block.

 24 Click on the green flag [] to run the game. Everything should work as before, but this time if you touch the robot the game will stop with a meow sound. If there's no meow, check that the sound volume is turned up on your computer and that you've used the version of the PLAY SOUND block that says "until done" at the end.

25 Now click on the full-screen button at the top left of the editor window to play the game without the distraction of seeing all the code to one side. Click on it again when you want to return to the normal screen view.

Click here to change to full-screen viewing.

Cargo Bay Chase
by ScruffyLookingNerfHerder (unshared)

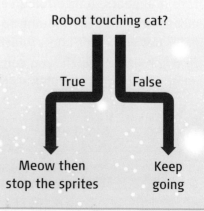 **C-3PO says...**

If-then

You make decisions every day. If you want to know the Death Star's weakness so you can destroy it, you'll need its plans. Computer programs also make decisions using what coders call conditional statements, such as "if-then". When Scratch reaches an IF-THEN block, the blocks inside the IF-THEN block are run only if the statement is true. If the statement is false, the inner blocks are skipped.

Robot touching cat?

True   False

Meow then stop the sprites   Keep going

Keeping score

Computer games often need to keep track of vital statistics, such as the player's score or health. These changing numbers are called "variables". To keep track of the player's score in Cargo Bay Chase, create a variable that counts the number of energy balls the player has collected.

 26 With any sprite selected, choose the orange DATA heading in the BLOCKS PALETTE. Click on the "Make a Variable" button.

Select the
DATA
BLOCKS
PALETTE

Click here to create a new variable.

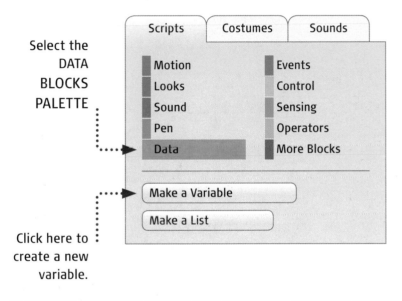

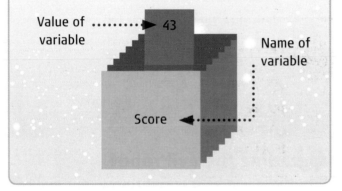

C-3PO says...

Variables

A variable is like a box in which you store information, such as a number, that can change. Variables are given names, such as "Score", and are used for storing numbers and other kinds of information, too. The information stored in the box is known as the variable's value. When naming variables, choose a name that tells you what the variable represents, such as "Speed" or "Score". Most computer languages won't let you put spaces in the names of variables, so a good tip is to combine words. Instead of using "Robot Speed", for example, type "RobotSpeed".

Value of variable → 43

Name of variable

Score

---

27 A pop-up box appears asking you to give your variable a name. Type "CatScore" in the box. Make sure the option "For all sprites" is selected and hit "OK".

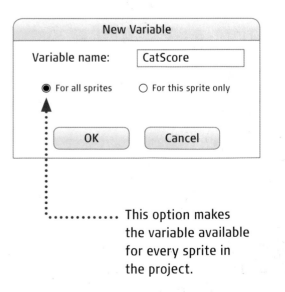

This option makes the variable available for every sprite in the project.

28 You'll see a set of new blocks appear, including one labelled "CatScore". Make sure the box next to it is ticked. This will show the score on the STAGE.

This box must be ticked.

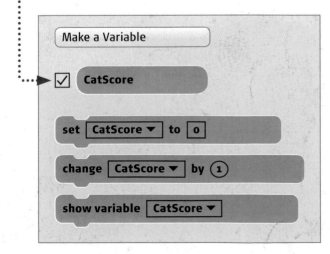

29 The score counter will appear in the top-left corner of the STAGE, but you can drag it anywhere you like.

Cargo Bay Chase
by ScruffyLookingNerfHerder (unshared)

CatScore   0

You can use the mouse to move the score display.

30 The score ("CatScore") should start at zero and increase by one each time the cat touches a ball. Select the Ball sprite and add the two orange DATA blocks (shown on the right) to its script. The first resets "CatScore" and the second increases it by one.

when ⚑ clicked

set CatScore ▼ to 0 ◄········

forever

    wait until   touching Cat ▼ ?

    change CatScore ▼ by 1 ◄·········

    play sound pop ▼

    go to random position ▼

    point in direction   pick random -179 to 180

This block sets the score to zero at the start of the game.

This block increases the score by one whenever the cat catches a ball.

31 Now click the green flag [⚑] to run the script and see what happens when the cat collects each ball. Can you collect 20 balls without bumping into the robot?

Upgrading the evil robot

With the game as it is right now, our evil robot can chase the energy ball, but nothing happens if the robot touches it. Follow these next steps to fix that.

32 Click on the Ball sprite to select it in the SPRITES LIST and add this third script so that the ball moves to a new position when the robot touches it.

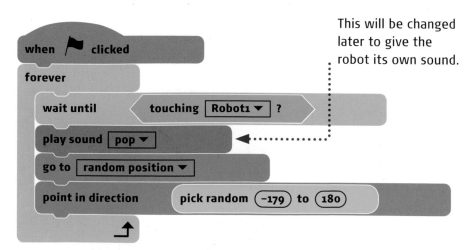

when ⚑ clicked

forever

    wait until   touching Robot1 ▼ ?

    play sound pop ▼

    go to random position ▼

    point in direction   pick random -179 to 180

This will be changed later to give the robot its own sound.

33 Run the project and let the robot catch the energy ball. The ball should disappear, then reappear somewhere else. If it doesn't, check your script carefully for errors.

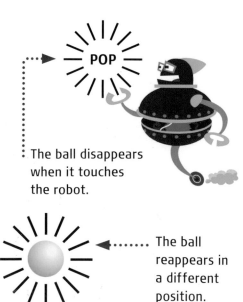

POP

The ball disappears when it touches the robot.

The ball reappears in a different position.

34 Next, add a new sound for when the robot collects the energy ball. Select the ball in the SPRITES LIST, then click on the SOUNDS tab at the top of the Scratch editor to see the sounds already loaded for this sprite. In the NEW SOUND menu, click on the speaker icon [🔊] to access the sound library.

Clicking on this tab shows you which sounds have been loaded for the sprite you've selected. ....

Scripts	Costumes	Sounds

New sound:

Click on the speaker icon to open the Scratch sound library.

You have learned much, young one.

35 In the sound library, you'll see lots of sound samples that you can use. Find the "boing" sound and click on it. Then click "OK". The "boing" sound will appear in the list of the Ball sprite's sounds.

boing
00:00.30

This is the length of the sound in hours, minutes and seconds. The "boing" sound is 0.30 seconds long.

36 Now go back to the Ball sprite's scripts by clicking the SCRIPTS tab at the top of the Scratch editor. Find the script that reacts to touching the robot, then click on the drop-down menu in the PLAY SOUND block to select the new sound.

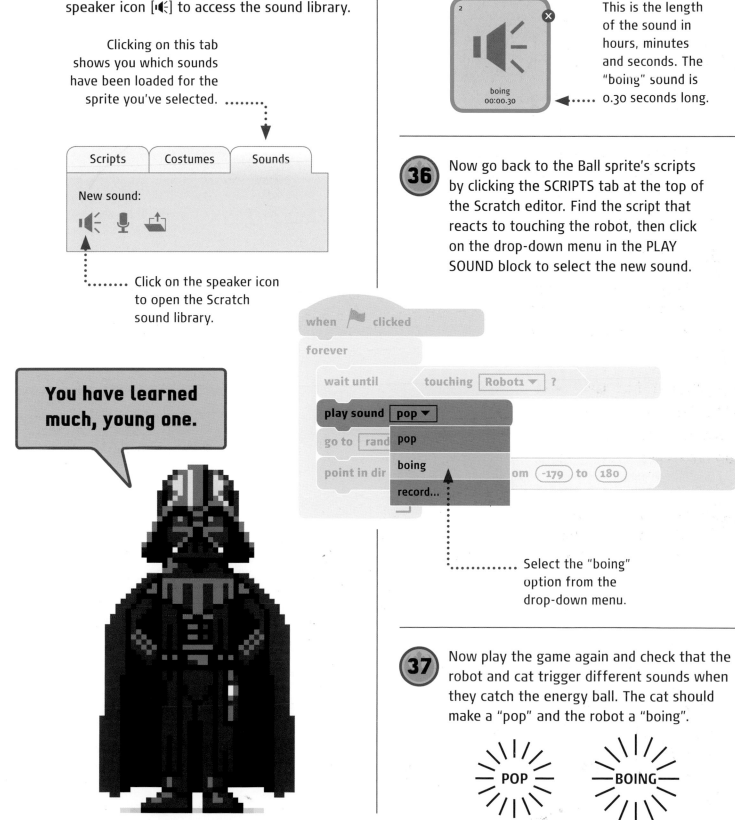

when 🏴 clicked

forever

wait until   touching Robot1 ▼ ?

play sound pop ▼

go to rand   pop

point in dir   boing   om (-179) to (180)

record...

Select the "boing" option from the drop-down menu.

37 Now play the game again and check that the robot and cat trigger different sounds when they catch the energy ball. The cat should make a "pop" and the robot a "boing".

POP   BOING

Faster, evil robot, faster!

The game is fun, but it's easy to amass an enormous score without the robot getting much of a look in. What if every time the robot captured an energy ball it got more power and could move faster?

Enter the variable's name in this box. Click "OK" to create the variable.

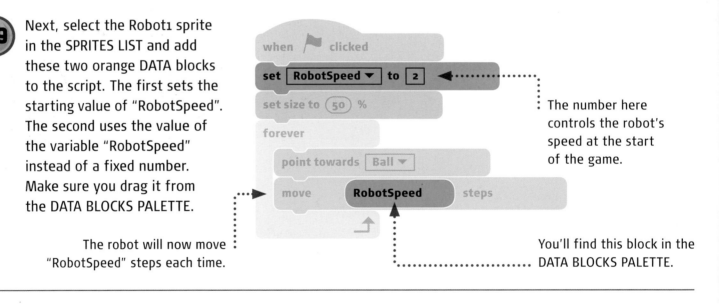

38 At present, the robot moves at a constant speed, but it's easy to change that using a variable. Go to the DATA BLOCKS PALETTE and create a new variable called "RobotSpeed" to control how many steps the robot takes. The new variable will appear on the STAGE – don't worry, you can hide it later.

New Variable

Variable name: RobotSpeed

● For all sprites   ○ For this sprite only

OK   Cancel

39 Next, select the Robot1 sprite in the SPRITES LIST and add these two orange DATA blocks to the script. The first sets the starting value of "RobotSpeed". The second uses the value of the variable "RobotSpeed" instead of a fixed number. Make sure you drag it from the DATA BLOCKS PALETTE.

when ⚑ clicked
set RobotSpeed ▼ to 2
set size to 50 %
forever
  point towards Ball ▼
  move RobotSpeed steps

The number here controls the robot's speed at the start of the game.

The robot will now move "RobotSpeed" steps each time.

You'll find this block in the DATA BLOCKS PALETTE.

40 Run the project. The robot should still chase the ball, but this time more slowly. To make the evil robot speed up each time it touches an energy ball, select the ball in the SPRITES LIST and add this extra block to the script used to detect collisions between the robot and the ball. This new block increases the value of "RobotSpeed" by one with each collision.

when ⚑ clicked
forever
  wait until touching Robot1 ▼ ?
  play sound boing ▼
  go to random position ▼
  point in direction pick random -179 to 180
  change RobotSpeed ▼ by 1

This number controls how much the robot speeds up with each ball it collects.

41 Now try the game again. The robot should speed up, but it will become amazingly fast in almost no time at all! You'll see a rapid increase in the value of "RobotSpeed" displayed on the STAGE. Change the 1 in the new block to 0.2, so there's less acceleration each time, then run the game once more.

when 🏳 clicked
forever
    wait until   touching Robot1 ▼ ?
    play sound boing ▼
    go to random position ▼
    point in direction   pick random −179 to 180
    change RobotSpeed ▼ by 0.2

Change the robot's acceleration to 0.2.

---

42 You don't need to see the value of "RobotSpeed" on the STAGE. To make things tidy, select the orange DATA BLOCKS PALETTE and untick the box beside the "RobotSpeed" variable to hide it.

Tick: Show on STAGE

Untick: Don't show on STAGE

Make a Variable

☑ CatScore

☐ RobotSpeed

Time to play!

Well done – you've made your first Scratch game. Play it a few times to check that it all works as it should, then challenge your friends to a competition. If you find the game too easy or too hard, don't be afraid to change the speed or size of the sprites to adjust the difficulty level. Watch others play to see if you've got the settings right.

when 🏳 clicked
point in direction   pick random −179 to 180
forever
    move 10 steps
    if on edge, bounce

Make this number bigger to speed up the ball. Make it smaller to slow the ball down.

You can adjust the cat's size by altering the value of the SET SIZE block in the cat's script.

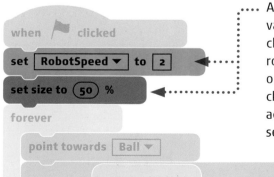
when 🏳 clicked
set RobotSpeed ▼ to 2
set size to 50 %
forever
    point towards Ball ▼

Alter these values to change the robot's speed or size. To change its acceleration, see step 40.

when 🏳 clicked
set size to 50 %
forever
    go to mouse-pointer ▼
    if   touching Robot1 ▼ ?   then

Make the game your own

Now you've got your game working, you can experiment. Make your version of the game unique with changing colours, extra characters or different sprites and sounds. You can also add a high score display to help decide who's the best player.

Save a copy of the game

If you're working online, go to the File menu and select the "Save as a copy" option. If you're working offline, you can select "Save as" and give the project a new name. That way, you'll have a safe copy of the game that you can go back to, leaving you free to experiment.

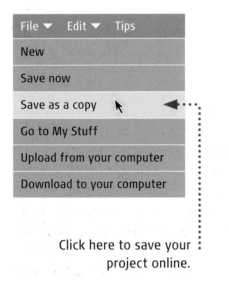

File ▼   Edit ▼   Tips
New
Save now
Save as a copy
Go to My Stuff
Upload from your computer
Download to your computer

File ▼   Edit ▼   Tips
New
Open
Save
Save as
Record Project Video
Share to website

Click here to save your project online.

Click here to save your project offline.

Make the ball change colour

It's easy to make the energy ball change colour as it bounces around. Add this short script with a CHANGE COLOR EFFECT block from the purple LOOKS BLOCKS PALETTE. You can add this script to any sprite or backdrop to make it flash with colour.

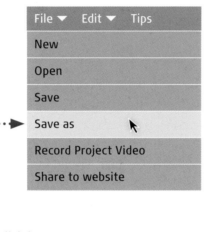

```
when 🏳 clicked
forever
    change [color ▼] effect by (5)
```

The larger this number, the faster the ball will change colour.

Remember, the Force will be with you... always.

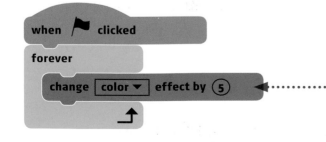

C-3PO says...

Debugging
Something not working? A bug in your program? Try these tips.

➤ Check your scripts. Have you omitted or mixed up blocks? (POINT TOWARDS and GO TO are often confused.) Did you choose the wrong drop-down option or put the wrong number somewhere? Are blocks where they should be inside or outside a loop or an IF-THEN block?

➤ Tick the variables to display them on the STAGE. If the values aren't what you expect, it might give you a clue as to what and where the problem is.

➤ Ask someone else to help you check your code – they may spot something you've missed.

Choose some background music

The STAGE can have its own scripts and sounds, which makes it easy to add background music to the game. Click on the small copy of the STAGE at the bottom left of the Scratch editor, then on the SOUNDS tab to load a music loop from the library.

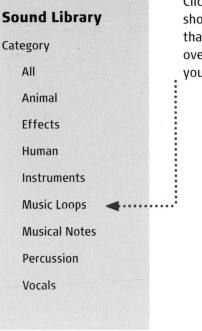

Sound Library

Category

All

Animal

Effects

Human

Instruments

Music Loops ◄ ∙∙∙∙∙∙∙∙∙∙∙

Musical Notes

Percussion

Vocals

Click on "Music Loops" to show all the sound clips that can be played over and over. Choose a music loop you like, then click "OK".

Click the play button on a library sample to listen to the loop before you load it.

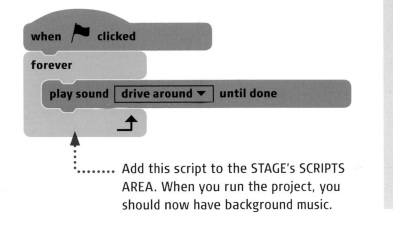

Add this script to the STAGE's SCRIPTS AREA. When you run the project, you should now have background music.

Show the highest score

Create a new variable called "HighScore" and leave it showing on the STAGE. Then add these blocks to the section of the Cat sprite's script that ends the game. Any new high score will now be automatically updated and displayed on the STAGE.

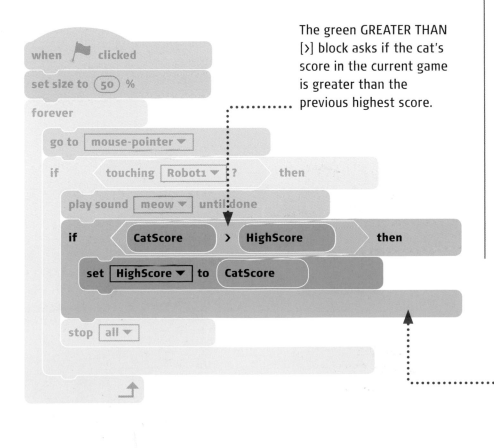

The green GREATER THAN [>] block asks if the cat's score in the current game is greater than the previous highest score.

This IF-THEN block saves a new "Highscore" value if the player has beaten it in the current game.

Give it a twist

Can you think of new twists for the game? Maybe change the way the ball moves or modify the cat's controls so that it chases the mouse-pointer instead of sticking to it? How about adding another sprite that chases the cat and makes life more difficult? Think about the steps to add the robot to the game and adapt them for the new character.

New theme

Later on you'll learn how to make your own sprites and sound clips. Once you've mastered these skills, you can change the theme of this project with your own creations.

Build-a-Droid

Anakin Skywalker is great at making droids. Why not take him on and create your own droid workshop? For this project, you'll find or design each droid part so that by the end, you'll be a master Scratch sprite creator! Time to get your toolbox out.

Aim of the game

Each droid starts with a main body unit on the workbench – use the space bar to choose one from the selection available. Then drag and drop body parts from the storage area onto the main body to create your own unique droid. You can also add scripts to animate body parts so they move or change shape. This project works best in full-screen mode.

How to build the game

Each body part is a sprite that you'll need to create. There are different ways to get pictures for these sprites, which are also known as "costumes". This chapter guides you through all the ways to create your own sprites.

Click here to hide the code and build droids in full-screen mode.

Scratch libraries Scratch's sprite and costume libraries have lots of images you can use without restrictions.

Build-a-Droid
by DroidMaker (unshared)

Sprite mods You can edit Scratch's built-in costumes with the paint editor to make something new.

Storage area This part of the STAGE is full of droid parts, ready to be used in new creations.

Use the mouse-pointer to drag and drop parts from the storage area onto your workbench.

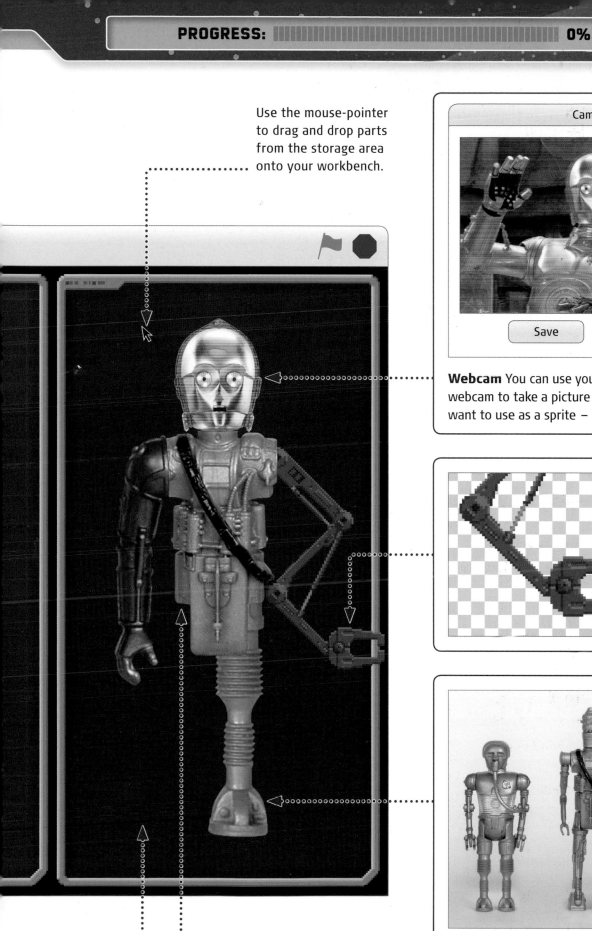

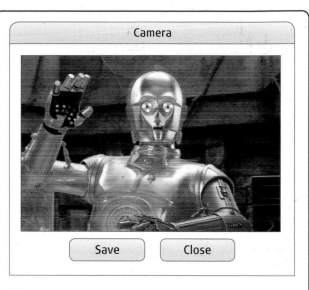

Camera

Save   Close

Webcam You can use your computer's webcam to take a picture of something you want to use as a sprite – like yourself!

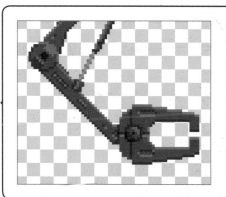

Drawing You can draw your own sprites using Scratch's built-in paint editor.

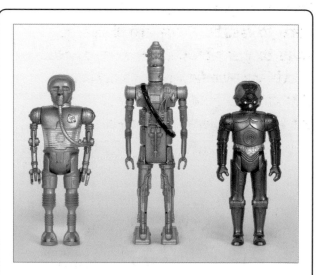

Photo Upload your own photos, find copyright-free images from the internet or scan your own drawings. If you don't want a whole image, you can cut out areas using the paint editor.

Workbench This is where you combine body parts to create unique droids.

Every droid starts with one of many body units. Press the space bar to switch between the options.

Drawing sprites

Start your droid parts collection with a sprite you've drawn yourself using the Scratch paint editor.

1 Start a new project and name it "Build-a-Droid". Remove the Cat sprite by right-clicking on it in the SPRITES LIST and selecting "Delete". To make your own sprite, click on the paintbrush icon [/] in the NEW SPRITE menu, above the SPRITES LIST.

New sprite:

Click here to open the paint editor.

C-3PO says...

Costumes

A costume is a picture a sprite can show on the STAGE. One sprite can have several costumes and can switch between them when a script tells it to.

3 A droid's body can be as simple as a circle. Choose the ellipse tool. Click and move the mouse-pointer to pull out a circle or oval. If you want a perfect circle, hold down the Shift key.

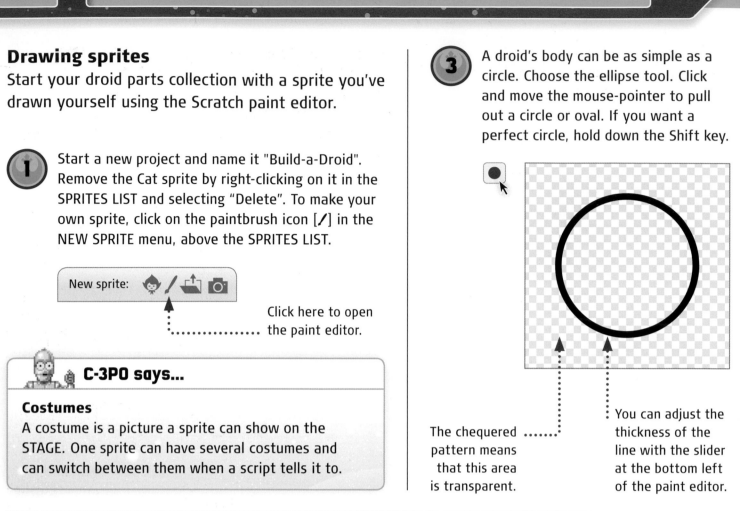

The chequered pattern means that this area is transparent.

You can adjust the thickness of the line with the slider at the bottom left of the paint editor.

2 Scratch's paint editor will now open. Make sure "Bitmap Mode" is selected in the bottom-right corner.

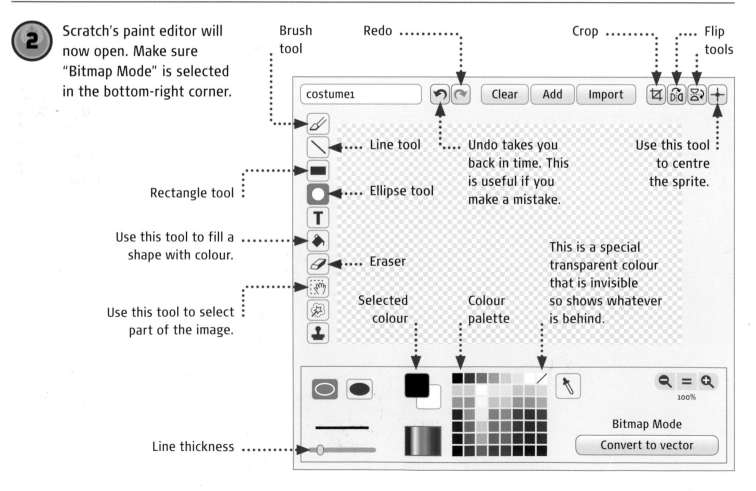

Brush tool

Redo

Crop

Flip tools

Line tool

Undo takes you back in time. This is useful if you make a mistake.

Use this tool to centre the sprite.

Rectangle tool

Ellipse tool

Use this tool to fill a shape with colour.

Eraser

This is a special transparent colour that is invisible so shows whatever is behind.

Use this tool to select part of the image.

Selected colour

Colour palette

Line thickness

4 Now choose the fill tool, which looks like a bucket of paint being tipped over []. Click in the colour palette at the bottom to choose a colour for the body. Then click inside the circle to fill it with your chosen colour.

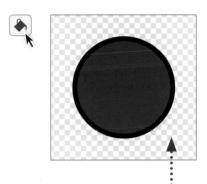

The background should still show the "transparent" chequered pattern.

5 If you want to add details to your droid body, click on the brush tool [✐] in the upper-left corner of the paint editor. Choose a colour and click to draw the details on the body. Use the fill tool to colour in any solid areas. If the colour accidentally fills an unwanted area, click the undo button and check the lines for any gaps.

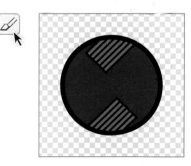

6 Look across at the sprite on the STAGE. Is it too big or too small? You can click on the grow or shrink tools at the top of the Scratch screen and then click on the sprite.

Grow tool ..... Shrink tool

7 Now check where Scratch thinks the centre of the sprite is by clicking the set costume centre tool [✛], found in the top-right corner. A cross will appear on the paint editor. Drag the cross to the centre of your sprite.

Set costume centre tool

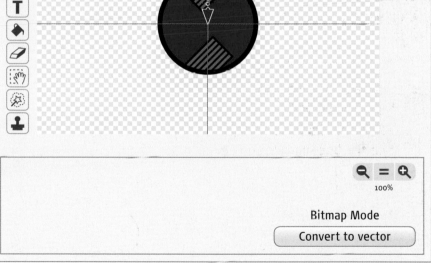

costume1   Clear   Add   Import

.... The sprite's centre

100%

Bitmap Mode
Convert to vector

8 Well done – you've created a droid body! As a finishing touch, click the blue "i" icon on this sprite in the SPRITES LIST and change the name to "Body" in the information panel. Click the back arrow to save the sprite's name.

Change name here

Back arrow

Body
x: 84   **y:** -69   **direction:** -90°
rotation style: ↺ ↔ ●
can drag in player: ☐
show: ☑

9 When you run the project, every sprite will be positioned on the STAGE. To place your Body sprite on the workbench, on the right-hand side of the STAGE, click on the SCRIPTS tab and add this script.

```
when ⚑ clicked
go to x: 150 y: 0
```

.... This block sends the sprite to the right of the STAGE.

Build-a-Droid
by DroidMaker (unshared)

Using built-in sprites

The Scratch library has a selection of sprites and costumes. These are free and there are no restrictions on how they can be used.

10 To load a ready-made sprite, click on the sprite library button [♠] in the NEW SPRITE menu, just above the SPRITES LIST.

New sprite: 👩 / 🖌️ 📤 📷

Click here to open the sprite library.

11 The sprites are listed in alphabetical order. Click on the one you want to load and press the "OK" button at the bottom of the window. The sprite will appear in the SPRITES LIST. Don't forget you can use the shrink and grow tools to resize any sprite.

Glasses   Headband

For this project "Glasses" and "Headband" will be useful sprites.

🤖 C-3PO says...

Coordinates

To pinpoint any spot on the STAGE you can use two numbers called coordinates. The x coordinate, written first, tells you how far the point is across the STAGE horizontally. The y coordinate, written second, tells you how far the point is up or down the STAGE vertically. The x coordinates go from –240 to 240. The y coordinates go from –180 to 180. The coordinates of a point are written as (x, y). The centre of C-3PO's head on the right, for instance, has coordinates (180, 135).

Every spot on the STAGE has a unique pair of coordinates ..... that can be used to position a sprite exactly.

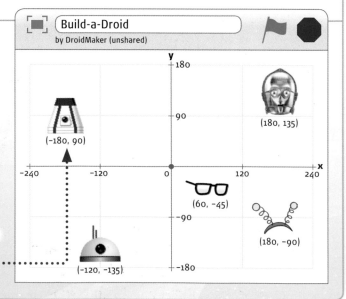

Build-a-Droid
by DroidMaker (unshared)

(−180, 90)

(180, 135)

(60, −45)

(180, −90)

(−120, −135)

12 Add a short script like this to each of your sprites so they appear in the storage area. If you drag the sprite to the desired location on the STAGE, the GO TO block in the BLOCKS PALETTE will automatically fill in the correct numbers for that position. Click on the blue "i" icon of each sprite to make sure that the "can drag in player" option is ticked. This ensures the project will work in full-screen mode.

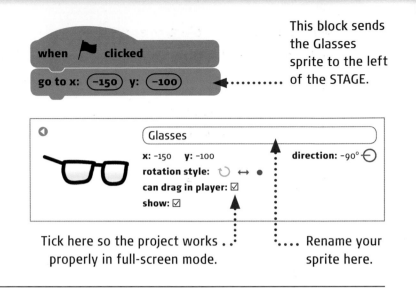

This block sends the Glasses sprite to the left of the STAGE.

Tick here so the project works properly in full-screen mode.

Rename your sprite here.

Modifying built-in sprites

You can also use built-in sprites as a base for your own drawings, for example, you can become a true droid mechanic by making a new droid head out of a ball!

13 Load the "Ball" sprite from the library. Click on the COSTUMES tab to access the paint editor. Follow the numbered steps below to convert the ball into a head. If you can't see the tools, check step 1.

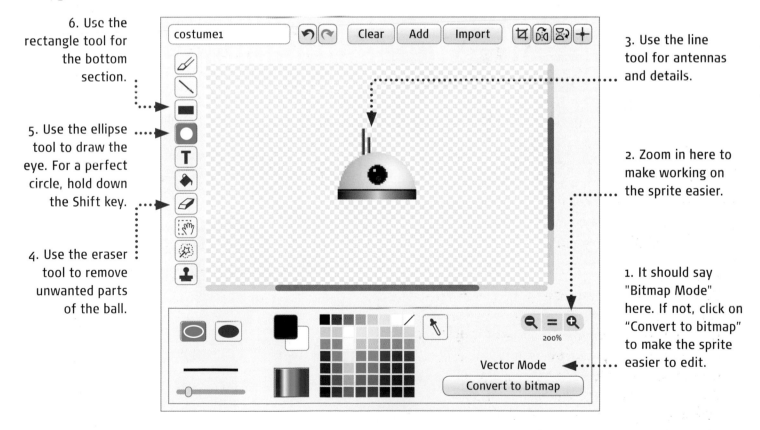

6. Use the rectangle tool for the bottom section.

5. Use the ellipse tool to draw the eye. For a perfect circle, hold down the Shift key.

4. Use the eraser tool to remove unwanted parts of the ball.

3. Use the line tool for antennas and details.

2. Zoom in here to make working on the sprite easier.

1. It should say "Bitmap Mode" here. If not, click on "Convert to bitmap" to make the sprite easier to edit.

14 Resize the sprite if you need to. Click on the blue "i" icon to rename it and check that the "can drag in player" box is ticked. Finally, add this script.

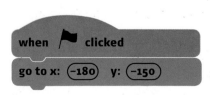

Using photos

Scratch gives you the tools to make sprites from your photos – or even parts of photos. These could be photos you've taken yourself or scans of drawings you've made. You can even use your computer's webcam to take pictures to use.

15 There are two different ways to import photos into Scratch. One way is for existing photos. The other is to take a new picture using the webcam. Both use buttons in the NEW SPRITE menu, which is found above the SPRITES LIST.

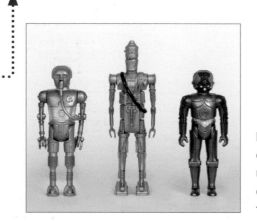

Click here to upload an existing photo.

New sprite:

Click here to use the webcam.

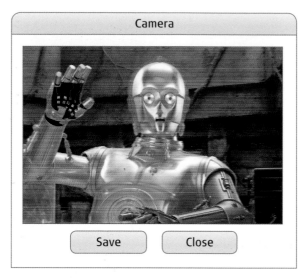

Camera

Save   Close

You can take pictures with your webcam. Just click the camera icon [📷] in the NEW SPRITE menu and click "Save" to make the picture you see into a new sprite.

If you have a picture on your computer you'd like to use, click the file icon [⬆] in the NEW SPRITE menu. You can use files in PNG, JPEG or GIF formats, but not BMP. You can also load SVG files, but make sure you click "Convert to bitmap" in the paint editor before you try to edit them.

C-3PO says...

Copyright and rights-free images
Be careful which photos you load into Scratch. Images that belong to other people or companies are copyrighted so should not be used in Scratch. You should only use work that you've created yourself and isn't copied from someone else, or images that are copyright-free, such as the sprites in the Scratch library or in other people's Scratch games.

Droid, please!

16 Once your photo is loaded into Scratch, you can cut out the parts you want. Click on the COSTUMES tab at the top of the screen to load the paint editor. Use the zoom tool to get a closer look at the part of the picture you want to cut out. Then click the magic wand tool, which helps you to remove unwanted parts of the picture.

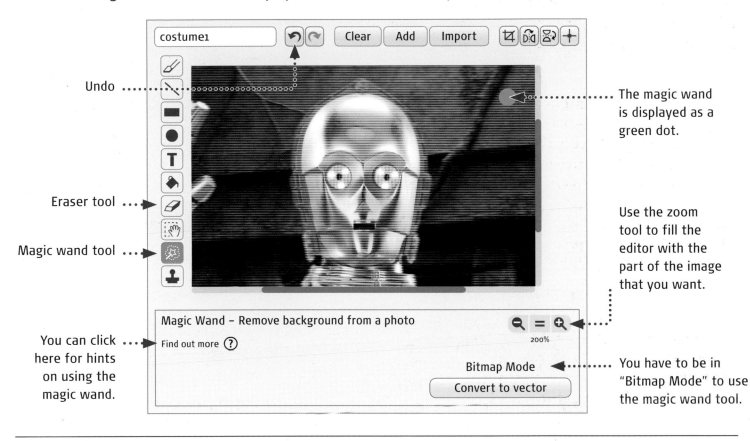

Undo

Eraser tool

Magic wand tool

The magic wand is displayed as a green dot.

Use the zoom tool to fill the editor with the part of the image that you want.

You can click here for hints on using the magic wand.

You have to be in "Bitmap Mode" to use the magic wand tool.

Hold the mouse-pointer and use the magic wand tool to draw a green loop around the part of the picture that you want to keep. Let go once you've gone all the way around.

Draw a line around the important part of the picture.

Scratch will now show you the parts of the picture it's going to keep. You can draw more green lines now if it's missed anything. Don't worry if some of the background is still there – you can remove it later.

Scratch will keep this part of the picture.

Now click on the eraser tool, and everything outside the line will disappear. Use the eraser to rub out unwanted items. If you use the eraser in small bursts, you can reverse any mistakes with the undo button.

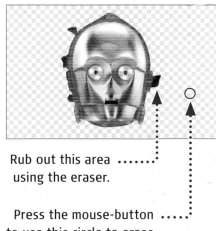

Rub out this area using the eraser.

Press the mouse-button to use this circle to erase parts of the picture.

17 You can adjust the size of the sprite by clicking on the shrink or grow tools at the top of the editor and then clicking on the sprite. Look on the STAGE to see the sprite's true size in case you're still zoomed in on the paint editor.

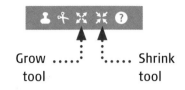

Grow ..... : ..... Shrink
tool   tool

 18 Now click on the set costume centre tool [+] and click in the middle of the sprite. This tells Scratch which point to use to position the sprite on the STAGE. This is the point that will be at the coordinates set in a GO TO block (see step 7).

 19 Now click on the blue "i" icon on this sprite in the SPRITES LIST and name the sprite. Also tick the "can drag in player" box so you can move the head when the game is in full-screen mode.

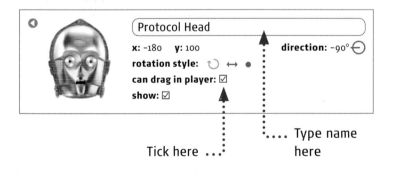

Tick here ... :   : .... Type name
                  here

 20 Well done! You have created your first salvaged droid part. Position this sprite in the storage area. Then click on the SCRIPTS tab and add this simple script. Remember: The GO TO block in the BLOCKS PALETTE will show the current coordinates of the sprite.

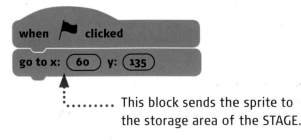

.... This block sends the sprite to the storage area of the STAGE.

Bringing everything together

Now that you know how to make your own droid parts, you can bring together everything you need for your workshop. This section shows you how to vary the main body piece, complete your sprite collection and decorate your workshop with a backdrop.

 21 To add costumes to your Body sprite, click on the COSTUMES tab and add bodies using the buttons in the NEW COSTUME menu. Another way to do this is to drag and drop a costume from another sprite onto the Body sprite.

These buttons add costumes to an existing sprite. They don't make a new sprite.

22 Once you have more than one costume for the body sprite, you can make the body shown on screen change to a different one when you press the space bar. Click on the SCRIPTS tab, select the body sprite in the SCRIPTS AREA and add this script.

When | space ▼ | key pressed

next costume

This block swaps a costume to the next one in the list, looping back to the beginning when necessary.

You'll find this block in the EVENTS BLOCK PALETTE.

23 Press the space bar. If the bodies don't all appear in the same spot on the STAGE, try resetting some of their centres (see step 7).

 24 Make the rest of your spare parts using the techniques already listed: drawing, using built-in sprites, adapting existing sprites and cutting out photos.

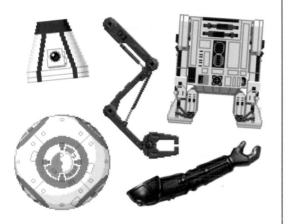

 25 Give each sprite a script to set its starting position and tick "can drag in player".

when ⚑ clicked

go to x: (-150) y: (100)

ⓘ can drag in player: ☑

 26 To add a backdrop to decorate the STAGE, click on the paintbrush icon [/] in the NEW BACKDROP menu. It's in the bottom-left corner of the Scratch editor, below a small picture of the STAGE.

Stage
1 backdrop

New backdrop:
🖼 / ⬆ 📷

27 Use your new drawing skills to create the outline of your workshop.

Use the rectangle or line tool in outline mode to draw the different areas of the backdrop.

Hit undo to reverse anything that you don't like.

backdrop1   ↩ ↪   Clear   Add   Import   ✄ 🔍 🔁

Bitmap Mode
Convert to vector

To add a background colour, use the fill tool.

Experiment with the different gradient fill tools.

You can even try out the text tool to make a sign for your workshop.

28 You should now have a fully functioning workshop! Run the project and all the parts should spring back to the correct positions in the storage area. Press the space bar to select a body, then drag parts on to it with the mouse. This project looks great in full-screen mode, but if you can't drag a part, check that you've selected "can drag in player" in the sprite's information panel (found by clicking the blue "i" icon on the sprite).

Animating sprites

You can have a lot of fun bringing your body-part sprites to life with animation. This can be done by writing extra code to move the sprite or creating additional costumes and switching between them.

 29 To make the round body roll, select the Body sprite in the SPRITES LIST and click on the SCRIPTS tab. Adapt the two existing scripts to these.

This block ensures that the costumes that don't spin are the right way up. ····▶

When [space ▼] key pressed

next costume

point in direction (90 ▼)

Drag this block from the LOOKS BLOCKS PALETTE.

This number should match the number of the costume that you want to apply this effect to.

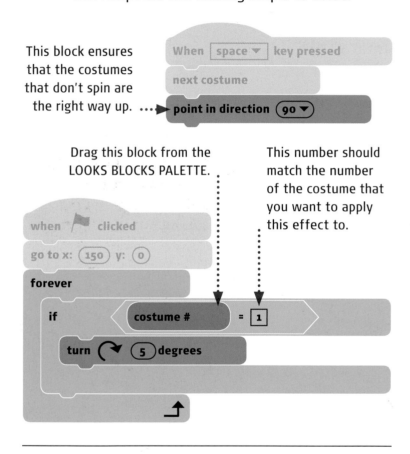

when 🏳 clicked

go to x: (150) y: (0)

forever

if 〈 costume # = 1 〉

  turn ↻ (5) degrees

 30 Run the project by clicking the green flag [🏳]. This will start the new FOREVER loop. Press the space bar to select the round body. Now it should look like it's rolling!

 31 If you've drawn an arm sprite, you can make it bend at the elbow. Select your arm sprite and click the COSTUMES tab. You can then make a copy of the arm costume by right-clicking and selecting the "duplicate" option.

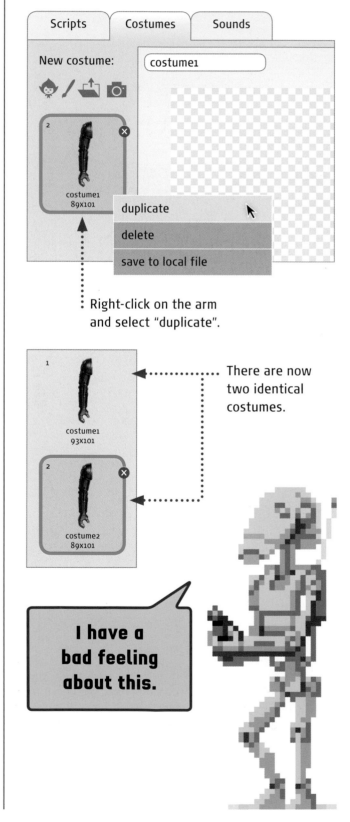

| Scripts | Costumes | Sounds |

New costume:

🧑/📤📷

costume1

2
costume1
89x101

duplicate

delete

save to local file

Right-click on the arm and select "duplicate".

1
costume1
93x101

2
costume2
89x101

There are now two identical costumes.

I have a bad feeling about this.

32 Select "costume2". Using the select tool, click and drag diagonally down to draw a box around the lower part of the arm, as shown below.

costume2   Clear   Add   Import

100%

Bitmap Mode

Convert to vector

33 Turn the selected part of the arm using the top circle on the selection box.

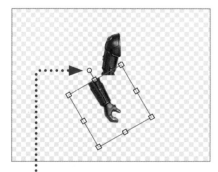

Click and drag this circle with the mouse to turn the contents of the box.

34 Move the lower portion of the arm using the centre circle so that it lines up with the rest of the arm.

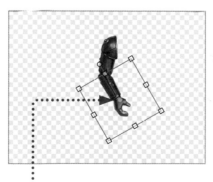

Drag this circle with the mouse-pointer and slide the lower arm to the right.

35 You now have two costumes in different positions. You can see them both on the costumes list.

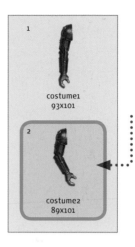

You may have to click to another sprite and back to this one to see the changes in the costumes list.

1   costume1   93x101

2   costume2   89x101

36 Now click on the SCRIPTS tab and add an extra script to the arm sprite to swap between the two costumes every second to animate the arm.

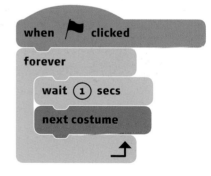

when ⚑ clicked

forever

   wait ① secs

   next costume

37 Run the project. The arm will bend and straighten on its own. You can add more positions by duplicating and editing the arm costume. Which other parts of your sprites will you animate?

38 You can wave a sprite using the TURN block from the MOTION BLOCKS PALETTE. In the paint editor, use the set costume centre tool [+] to change the centre of the sprite to be the point at which it attaches to the droid. Any TURN block will turn the sprite around this point.

39 Now add this extra script to wave the arm.

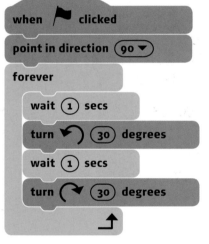

```
when [flag] clicked
point in direction (90 ▼)
forever
    wait (1) secs
    turn ↺ (30) degrees
    wait (1) secs
    turn ↻ (30) degrees
```

40 Run the project to see the arm wave to you. Why not experiment with different turning scripts?

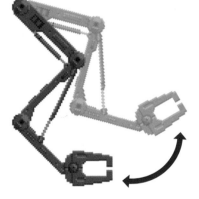

Artoo, you know better than to trust a strange computer!

Now try this!

This project is perfect for you to add your own ideas, drawings and code. You can even branch out into creating spaceships or aliens. Here are some ideas to get you started.

Reusable parts

You might want to use certain sprites multiple times – perhaps your droid would be better with seven arms rather than two? You can "clone" a sprite to make fully working copies. Make six clones of an arm sprite by adding this loop to its SCRIPTS AREA. Now when you run the project you can place all seven arms!

```
when [flag] clicked
go to x: (50) y: (50)
repeat (6)
    create clone of [myself ▼]
```

This block makes an identical copy of a sprite in exactly the same position on the STAGE.

This REPEAT loop creates six extra arms on top of the original.

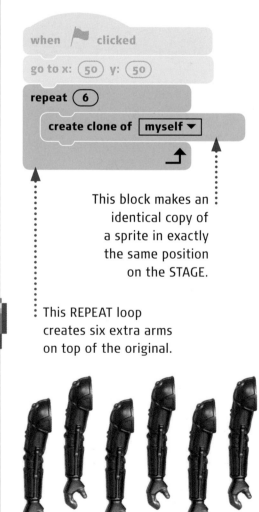

Colour changes

Add a script like this to any sprite to change the colour of that droid part at the touch of a button.

> **When** up arrow ▼ **key pressed**
> **change** color ▼ **effect by** (10)

The larger this number, the bigger the change in colour each time.

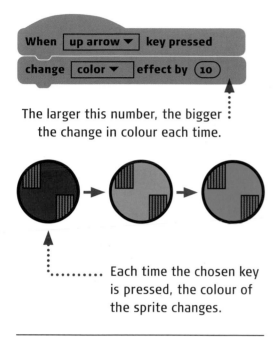

Each time the chosen key is pressed, the colour of the sprite changes.

Transparent parts

To make a part slightly see-through, add these blocks in the sprite's SCRIPTS AREA.

> **when** ⚑ **clicked**
> **change** ghost ▼ **effect by** (50)

This number can be 0 for solid to 100 for completely invisible!

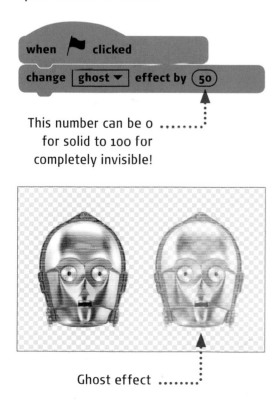

Ghost effect

These are not the droids we're looking for.

Import items from your other games

If you're using the online version of Scratch and you're logged in to your account, you can make use of the BACKPACK function to transfer sprites, costumes, backdrops and scripts between projects.

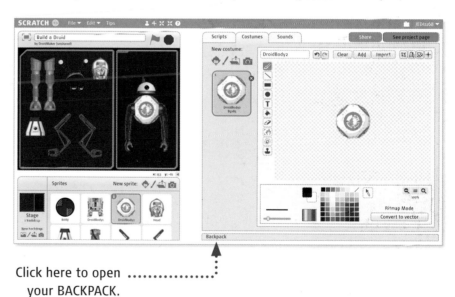

Click here to open your BACKPACK.

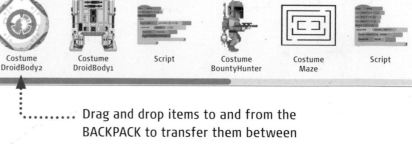

Drag and drop items to and from the BACKPACK to transfer them between all your different projects.

Jetpack Adventure

Ruthless bounty hunter Boba Fett wasn't able to become a master at using a jetpack without a lot of practice. Follow the steps in this project to build the ultimate jetpack training simulator. Have you got what it takes to be an efficient bounty hunter?

Aim of the game

As a bounty hunter on patrol, your mission is to keep going for as long as you can. But be careful: Without rocket boosts from your jetpack, you'll fall to the floor, but too much power and you'll disappear off the top of the STAGE. Squeeze through gaps in the barriers and make sure to pick up enough fuel supplies.

The meter shows how many fuel units are left.

The bounty hunter appears to fly forwards as the barriers scroll across the screen.

Jetpack Adventure
by RuthlessBountyHunter (unshared)

Fuel   68

timer   13.4

Game timer: How long can you survive?

The jetpack is boosted when the space bar is pressed.

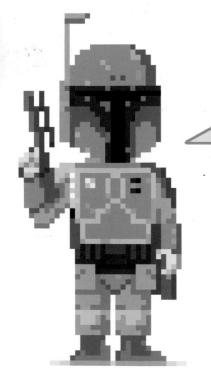

You should never underestimate my skills as a bounty hunter.

Draw a futuristic skyline for the backdrop.

Avoid the security barriers to stay alive.

Collect fuel to keep the jetpack running.

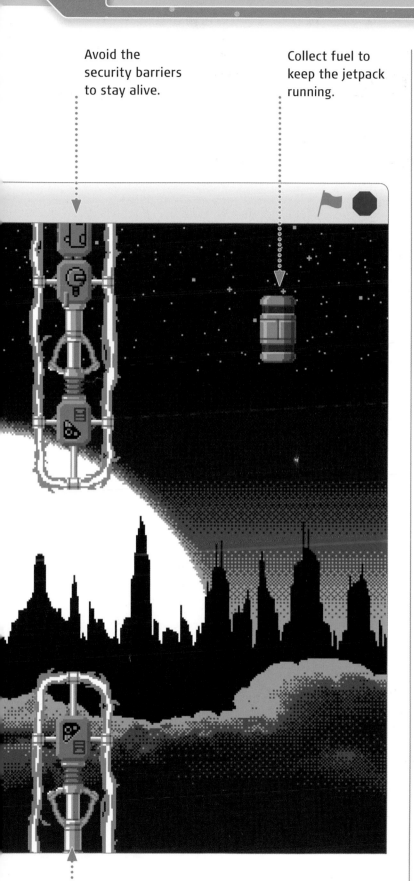

Barriers move from right to left while the bounty hunter moves up and down.

How to build the game

This game makes the Bounty Hunter sprite move as if gravity is pulling it down and the booster on the jetpack is pushing it upwards. Game programmers call this "game physics".

1 Start Scratch and create a new project. To get started, you can use the Cat sprite that's already loaded as your bounty hunter. You can turn him into a fully fledged bounty hunter later.

2 In this game the sprite will move up and down. To control this you need to make a variable called "Vspeed" to keep track of the sprite's vertical (up-down) speed. Choose the orange DATA BLOCKS PALETTE and click the "Make a Variable" button. Type "Vspeed" for the variable's name and hit "OK".

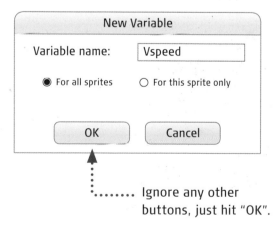

Ignore any other buttons, just hit "OK".

3 Make another two variables called "Gravity" and "Boost". "Gravity" will pull the jetpack down to the ground, whereas "Boost" will control the jetpack's power. Then add the script below to the Cat sprite to mimic gravity. Read the script through and try to figure out how it works.

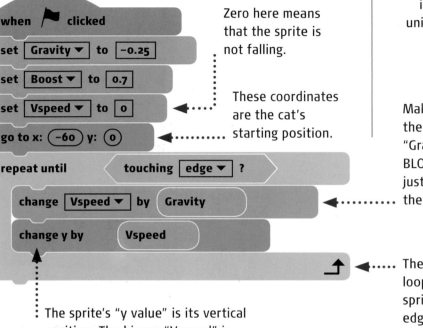

```
when  clicked
set  Gravity ▼  to  -0.25
set  Boost ▼  to  0.7
set  Vspeed ▼  to  0
go to x: -60  y: 0
repeat until          touching  edge ▼  ?
    change  Vspeed ▼  by  Gravity
    change y by  Vspeed
```

Zero here means that the sprite is not falling.

These coordinates are the cat's starting position.

Make sure you drag the block named "Gravity" from the BLOCKS PALETTE. If you just type in "Gravity", the script won't work.

The blocks inside this loop repeat until the sprite touches the edge of the STAGE.

The sprite's "y value" is its vertical position. The bigger "Vspeed" is, the further the sprite moves.

4 Now click the green flag [⚑] to run the script. The cat will start in the centre of the STAGE and fall with increasing speed to the floor. As the cat falls faster, watch the value of "Vspeed" become more negative in the window on the STAGE.

The cat speeds up as ⋯⋯▶ it falls. It falls one unit, then two units, then three units.

1

2

3

5 To avoid having to keep clicking the green flag to make the sprite fall, add a FOREVER loop around the main part of the code and insert a two-second delay. Run the project again and the sprite should fall, reset, then fall again. This coding will be useful later for making the game restart automatically.

```
when  clicked
set  Gravity ▼  to  -0.25
set  Boost ▼  to  0.7
forever
    set  Vspeed ▼  to  0
    go to x: -60  y: 0
    repeat until          touching  edge ▼  ?
        change  Vspeed ▼  by  Gravity
        change y by  Vspeed
    wait  2  secs
```

Drag and drop the FOREVER block here. It will surround all the blocks below it.

Type "2" here for a two-second delay. Make sure the WAIT block is after the end of the REPEAT UNTIL loop.

C-3PO says...

Avoid the bug!
When you use a variable inside another block, make sure you always drag the variable's orange block from the DATA BLOCKS PALETTE. Don't type the name of the variable yourself – your script won't work and it causes hard-to-spot errors.

 **C-3PO says...**

Repeat until

The useful REPEAT UNTIL loop repeats the blocks inside it until the condition at the top of the block becomes true, then the blocks below are run. This block makes it easier to write simple, readable code, like this example.

```
when 🏳 clicked

repeat until        touching  Sithlightsaber ▼

    duel

become one with the Force
```

Unlike the FOREVER block, REPEAT UNTIL has a bump at the bottom, allowing more blocks to be added to it.

6 Now add a boost to the jetpack whenever the space bar is pressed. Create this new section of code (an IF-THEN block with a block inside it) and insert it into the existing script for the cat.

```
repeat until        touching  edge ▼  ?

    if      key  space ▼  pressed?      then

        change  Vspeed ▼  by  Boost

    change  Vspeed ▼  by  Gravity
```

This IF-THEN block increases "Vspeed" by "Boost" when the space bar is pressed to give the sprite an upwards push.

7 Run the edited script by clicking the green flag [🏳]. Gravity still pulls the sprite down, but now a tap on the space bar will accelerate the sprite upwards again. The longer you hold the space bar, the faster the sprite will go up. See how long you can keep the sprite away from the edges of the STAGE by balancing the two forces.

Bring in the bounty hunter

It's time to replace the cat with a proper bounty hunter to make your game really come to life. You'll need three different costumes for the Bounty Hunter sprite so he can switch his appearance when different things happen to him.

8 Select the Cat sprite in the SPRITES LIST, then click the COSTUMES tab at the top of the screen. Select the paintbrush icon [/] in the NEW COSTUME menu to create a new, blank costume for you to edit in the paint editor. There are also other ways you can create your own costumes or sprites (see pages 14 and 15).

Type the name of each costume here.

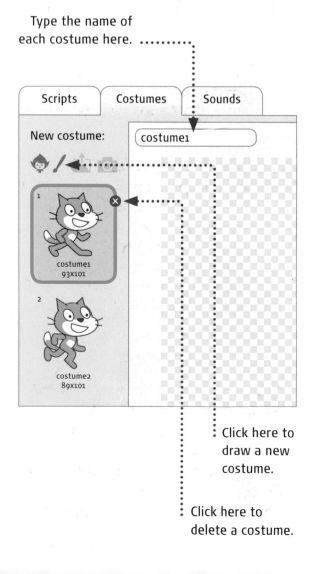

Click here to draw a new costume.

Click here to delete a costume.

9 Now you can design your own bounty hunter! You'll need to draw three costumes called "No Jet", "Jet" and "Shocked" (see below). Once you've made your costumes, delete the unwanted cat costumes. (Or, if you want to keep the cat, you can create cat versions of the costumes and use the shrink tool to reduce them to approximately 50 x 50 pixels.) Remember to centre your sprite with the set costume centre tool [+]. Also, look around your drawing for unwanted pixels, as they may stop the game from working properly.

New costumes (examples)

 **No Jet**
Size: 50 x 50 pixels

Purpose: Bounty hunter with his jetpack off.

Jet
Size: 50 x 50 pixels

Purpose: Bounty hunter with his jetpack in action.

 **Shocked**
Size: 50 x 50 pixels

Purpose: Bounty hunter when he's touched the edge or an obstacle. It means game over!

10 Click on the blue "i" icon on the selected sprite and rename the sprite "Bounty Hunter".

First click here to show all the sprite's details.

Next, click here and type "Bounty Hunter" to name the sprite.

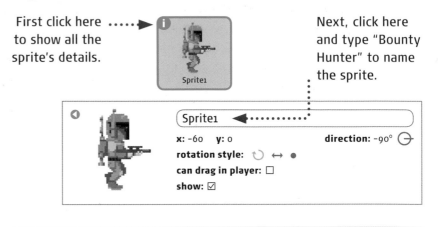

```
Sprite1
x: -60   y: 0                    direction: -90°
rotation style: ↻ ↔ •
can drag in player: ☐
show: ☑
```

11 Once you have your three costumes, update the bounty hunter's script to bring each costume into play. Add in a block for each costume so the game swaps between them at the right moment.

"No Jet" is the starting costume for the sprite.

```
go to x: -60 y: 0
repeat until            touching edge ▼ ?
    switch costume to No Jet ▼
    if      key space ▼ pressed?    then
        switch costume to Jet ▼
        change Vspeed ▼ by Boost

    change Vspeed ▼ by Gravity
    change y by        Vspeed

switch costume to Shocked ▼
wait 2 secs
```

When the space bar is pressed, you will see the jetpack fire.

When the bounty hunter touches the edge, the "Shocked" costume will appear.

12 Now run the project. The bounty hunter's jetpack should shoot out a jet of flame when the space bar is pressed. The sprite should also switch to the "Shocked" costume when he touches the edges of the STAGE. Try the full-screen button at the top left of the STAGE to see the game fill the screen.

See flames shoot out when the space bar is pressed.

Touching the edge of the STAGE shocks the bounty hunter.

Putting up barriers

With practice, it soon becomes too easy to pilot the bounty hunter to avoid the deadly edges of the STAGE. To add some challenge, make some obstacles that the bounty hunter must avoid. These deadly barriers, with just a small gap to fly through, move from right to left, across the screen towards the bounty hunter. This creates the effect of the bounty hunter flying to the right.

13 The barrier will be a new sprite. Click the paintbrush icon [/] in the NEW SPRITE menu, above the SPRITES LIST (not the paintbrush in the NEW COSTUME menu that you used earlier). The paint editor will open. Name the sprite "Barrier".

New sprite: 👧 / ⬆ 📷

Your sprite should be around 35 pixels wide and 360 pixels tall.

You can start with a simple barrier and decorate it later.

14 Paint your barrier so it's the full height of the screen, but isn't very wide. Leave a gap that the bounty hunter can fit through. This sprite will be scaled up to 150 per cent on screen so everything will get a bit bigger. If you like, you can start with a very simple barrier of two plain rectangles to get the game working and then make it more complicated later.

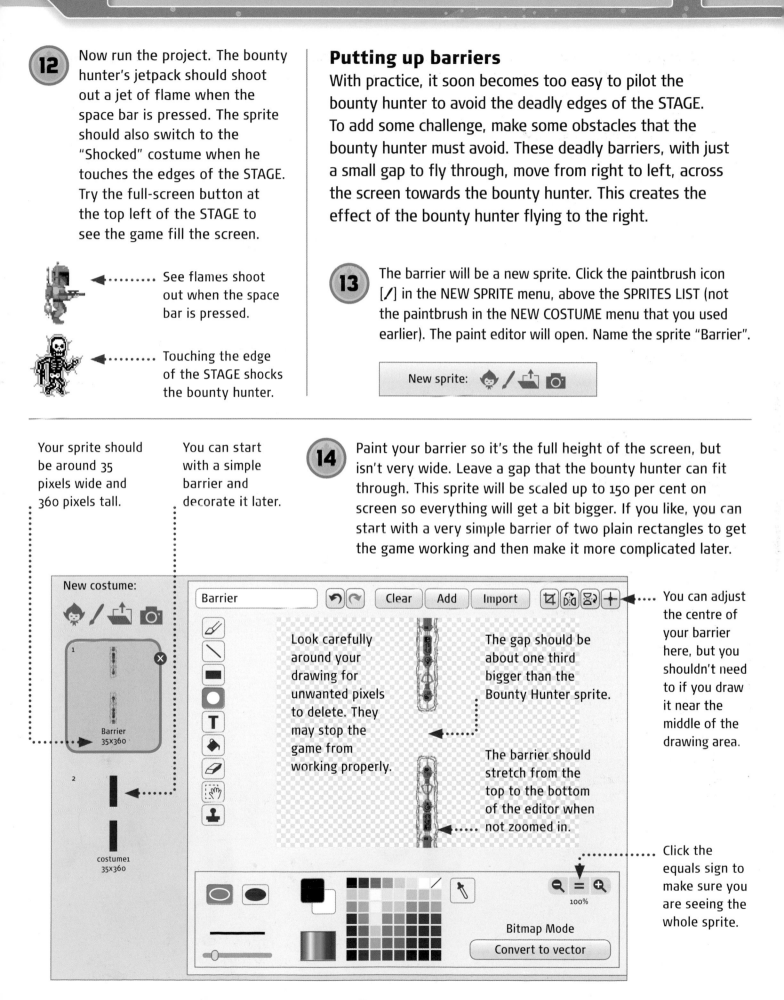

New costume:
👧 / ⬆ 📷

Barrier
35×360

costume1
35×360

Barrier

Clear　Add　Import

Look carefully around your drawing for unwanted pixels to delete. They may stop the game from working properly.

The gap should be about one third bigger than the Bounty Hunter sprite.

The barrier should stretch from the top to the bottom of the editor when not zoomed in.

You can adjust the centre of your barrier here, but you shouldn't need to if you draw it near the middle of the drawing area.

Click the equals sign to make sure you are seeing the whole sprite.

Bitmap Mode
Convert to vector

15 Now click on the SCRIPTS tab at the top of the screen and create a new variable "BarrierStep" (for all sprites). This will determine how many steps the barrier moves. Add this new script to the Barrier sprite so it moves from right to left across the STAGE.

The barrier moves 4 steps to the left each time.

Enlarging the barrier stops gaps from appearing above or below the sprite when it appears in higher or lower positions.

The barrier's starting position is on the right of the STAGE at a random height.

This REPEAT UNTIL loop moves the barrier left until it moves slightly off the left of the STAGE.

Switching the colours quickly makes the barrier look like it's electrified.

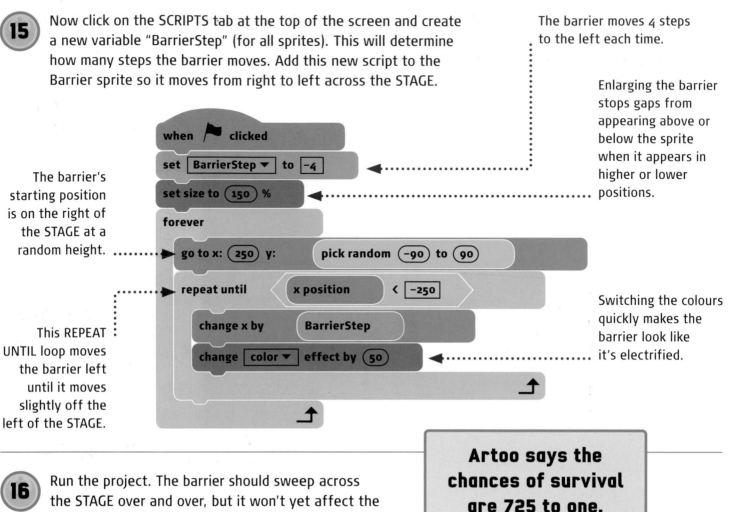

16 Run the project. The barrier should sweep across the STAGE over and over, but it won't yet affect the bounty hunter if it's touched. If the barrier gets stuck on the left-hand side of the screen and doesn't restart, check that the centre of the sprite is in the middle of the gap using the set costume centre tool [+] (see page 15). You can also adjust the "–250" value in the LESS THAN [<] block. Try "–240", then "–230" and so on until the barrier no longer sticks.

Artoo says the chances of survival are 725 to one.

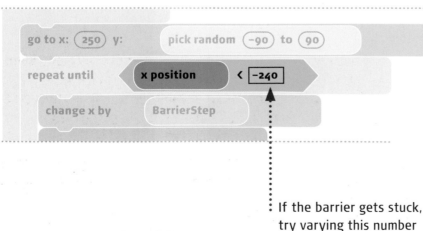

If the barrier gets stuck, try varying this number by intervals of 10.

17 To give your bounty hunter a shock when they bump into the barrier, select the Bounty Hunter sprite and edit this block of its script. Swap the TOUCHING EDGE block for an OR block with two TOUCHING options inside it. Now the game will end when the sprite touches either the edges of the STAGE or the new barriers.

The OR block ends the Bounty Hunter sprite's loop if either of the selected blocks are touched by the sprite.

go to x: (-60) y: (0)

repeat until ⟨ touching [edge ▼] ? ⟩ or ⟨ touching [Barrier ▼] ? ⟩

switch costume to [No Jet ▼]

18 Now you can sit back and play the game. Click the green flag [⚑] and see whether you can pilot the bounty hunter through the gaps without being frazzled. Try it in the full-screen mode for the full effect.

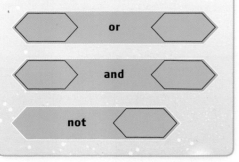

C-3PO says...

Complex tests
Sometimes you want to test for more than one condition. For example, in this game you need to test two conditions at once: "touching edge" or "touching barrier".

OR tests whether either condition is true. AND tests whether both conditions are true at the same time. The NOT block lets you check when something isn't happening.

⟨ ⟩ or ⟨ ⟩

⟨ ⟩ and ⟨ ⟩

not ⟨ ⟩

Adding fuel

Jetpacks don't run on fresh air – they need fuel! To add even more challenge to the game, you can make the bounty hunter dependent on collecting fuel canisters for the jetpack. If the fuel runs out, the bounty hunter will drop out of the sky.

19 Create a new sprite. You can draw your own or use a built-in sprite from Scratch. Name the sprite "Fuel". The bigger the Fuel sprite is, the easier collecting fuel will be. Remember to centre your sprite with the set costume centre tool [+] and look carefully around your drawing for unwanted pixels, as they may stop the game from working properly.

New sprite

Fuel
Size: 50 x 50 pixels

Purpose: Fuel canisters keep your jetpack running.

20 Add a variable called "Fuel" to keep track of how many units of fuel are in the bounty hunter's jetpack. Untick all the other variables. This will leave "Fuel" displayed on the STAGE so the player knows how much fuel is left in the tank.

A check here makes the variable appear in the game. ·······

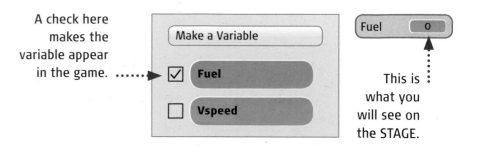

Make a Variable

☑ **Fuel**

☐ **Vspeed**

Fuel   0

This is what you will see on the STAGE.

21 Add this new script to the Fuel sprite to make the canisters appear randomly and track left across the screen. The script works in the same way as the barrier code except it hides the fuel most of the time.

The fuel is mostly hidden.

Fuel canisters appear after a random delay and at a random height.

Fuel disappears when the bounty hunter touches it. Make sure the IF-THEN block is inside the REPEAT UNTIL loop, not after it.

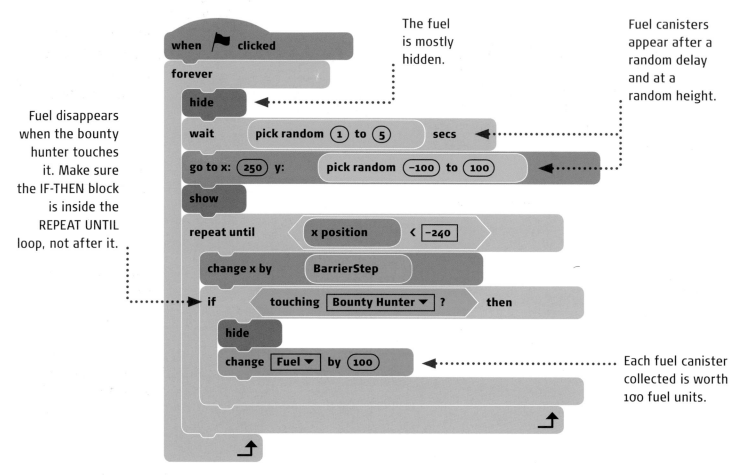

```
when [flag] clicked
forever
    hide
    wait (pick random (1) to (5)) secs
    go to x: (250) y: (pick random (-100) to (100))
    show
    repeat until < x position < -240 >
        change x by BarrierStep
        if < touching [Bounty Hunter ▼] ? > then
            hide
            change [Fuel ▼] by (100)
```

Each fuel canister collected is worth 100 fuel units.

22 Click the green flag [⚑] to check that the bounty hunter can collect the fuel by touching it while flying. You should see an extra 100 fuel units added to the display each time. However, the bounty hunter isn't using any fuel yet. Select the Bounty Hunter sprite and make these changes to the script so that the jetpack starts with some fuel and uses it up as it thrusts.

Drag the block named "Fuel" from the DATA BLOCKS PALETTE.

```
forever
    set [Fuel ▼] to [200]
    set [Vspeed ▼] to [0]
```

Add this block so the player always starts with 200 units of fuel.

```
switch costume to [No Jet ▼]
if < key [space ▼] pressed? > and < Fuel > [0] > then
    switch costume to [Jet ▼]
    change [Vspeed ▼] by (Boost)

change [Fuel ▼] by (-1)
```

Fuel units decrease by one every time the jetpack is used.

The jetpack only works if there are fuel units and the space bar is pressed.

23 Try the game again. Check whether you stay in the air if you collect fuel, but fall out of the sky when you use up all your fuel units (when your fuel reading reaches zero).

24 To add an atmospheric background picture, click on the paintbrush icon [/] in the NEW BACKDROP menu found in STAGE INFO in the bottom-left corner. Or you can click the library icon [🖼] to choose a built-in backdrop, such as "night city".

Stage
1 backdrop

New backdrop:
🖼 / ⬆ 📷

Click here to choose from .... Scratch's built-in backdrops.

Click here to draw your own backdrop. ....

 25 The fill tool can be used to create impressive horizon effects. You can also draw some futuristic buildings so the game feels like it's set on a distant planet.

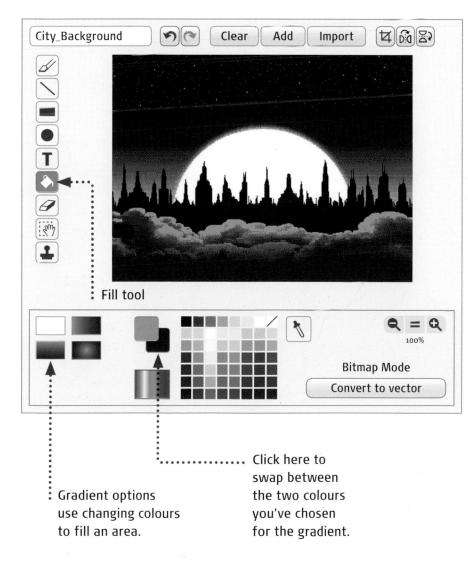

City_Background   ↺ ↻   Clear   Add   Import   🗗 🔳 🔲

Fill tool

Bitmap Mode
Convert to vector

Gradient options
use changing colours
to fill an area.

Click here to
swap between
the two colours
you've chosen
for the gradient.

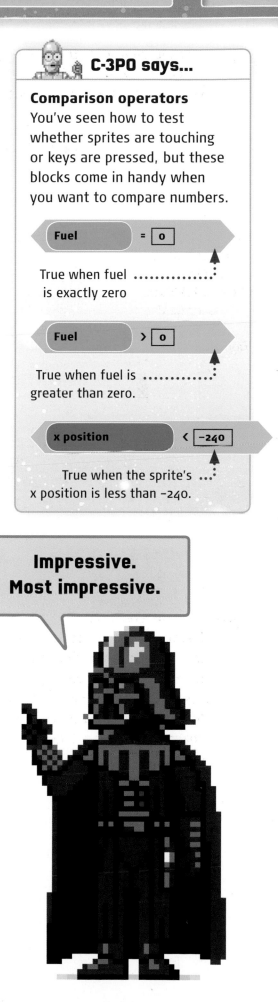

C-3PO says...

Comparison operators
You've seen how to test whether sprites are touching or keys are pressed, but these blocks come in handy when you want to compare numbers.

Fuel = 0

True when fuel .... is exactly zero

Fuel > 0

True when fuel is .... greater than zero.

x position < -240

True when the sprite's ...: x position is less than -240.

**Impressive.
Most impressive.**

Are you the best bounty hunter?

So far you've made a great game, but there's no way to tell how you're doing as a bounty hunter. Follow these instructions to use Scratch's built-in timer to measure how many seconds you survive. You can also add a display of your last and best times.

 26 Create two new variables named "BestTime" and "LastTime". Leave them ticked, so they appear on the STAGE. "BestTime" is the longest time anyone has managed to stay alive. "LastTime" is the score from the most recent game.

27 Click on the Bounty Hunter sprite and select the light-blue SENSING BLOCKS PALETTE. Find the oval TIMER block and tick it so its value appears on the STAGE. The value shown is the number of seconds since the timer was last reset. Scratch updates this for you automatically.

28 Arrange the "Fuel" and "Timer" variables in the top left-hand corner of the STAGE and "LastTime" and "BestTime" in the top right-hand corner.

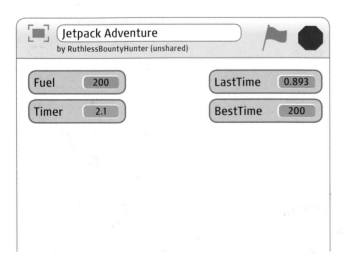

29 Add the RESET TIMER block near the start of the bounty hunter's script as shown below. This will set the timer to zero at the start of each game.

Insert the RESET TIMER block here.

30 Add these blocks near the end of the script to set the last and best times.

The "BestTime" is only reset if the last run was longer.

Make sure the WAIT block is after the IF-THEN block, not inside it.

31 Well done. Your game is now complete! Click the green flag [⚑] and compete with your friends to see who is the most agile bounty hunter.

Now try this!

You've built a great game and honed your skills as a jetpack pilot. Now it's time to prove your skills as a Scratch coder. Make a copy of the game (see page 32) and see how you can change the game with your own ideas!

Make some noise

The vacuum of space can be very silent, but to give your jetpack planet a little more atmosphere why not add some music and sound effects? To add music load up a music loop from the Scratch sound library (see page 33) and make a script to play the music.

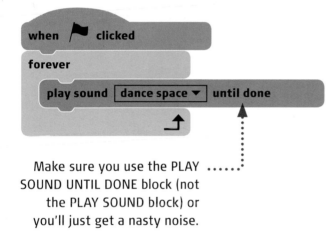

Make sure you use the PLAY SOUND UNTIL DONE block (not the PLAY SOUND block) or you'll just get a nasty noise.

To work out which sprite you need to load your chosen sound into, you'll need to figure out where the PLAY SOUND block needs to go in the code. The block needs to go at the point where an event happens. For example, a scream would go next to the costume change for the bounty hunter getting shocked. Don't be afraid to experiment.

Don't use the UNTIL DONE version of this SOUND block this time or the game will slow down.

Level up!

As you get better at flying a jetpack, you can easily change the difficulty level. The easiest settings to adjust are the power of the jetpack, the strength of gravity and the speed of the barriers. Just change the numbers a little in these blocks and see what happens to the game's playability. Can you make the barriers gradually speed up?

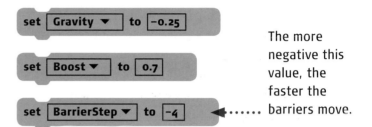

The more negative this value, the faster the barriers move.

You can also adjust how much fuel the jetpack starts with, how much it uses and how many fuel units there are in each collected fuel pack. Look for the blocks that set and change the fuel, and figure out what each one does.

> I use any means necessary to get the job done!

Use the Force!

Imagine moving something on screen purely by pointing your hand at it, like a Jedi does. This game lets you do just that! Instead of using a mouse or the keypad, you wave your arm – or move your whole body – just as though you're using the power of the Force. Welcome to the Jedi Temple, Padawan, for your first lesson in channelling the Force.

Aim of the game

Kyber crystals are rare gems that channel the Force and are used in lightsabers. They come in many colours, but beware the red ones. They channel the dark side of the Force, which makes them unstable and dangerous. In this game, you create your own crystals and then collect as many as you can by moving your arms and using a webcam. The Force may be with you, but it's a battle against the clock: You only have 30 seconds!

My ally is the Force, and a powerful ally it is.

This project works best in full-screen mode.

Boost your score by one point for every blue crystal you collect.

The timer counts down from 30 seconds.

Use the Force!
by JediPadawan1138

Score   19

Countdown   18

Collect the blue crystals that appear at random on the STAGE.

Each red crystal the training pod touches costs you five points.

Use your hands or body to control the training pod via the webcam.

You will see yourself in the background of the game.

How to build the game

To feel like you're really channelling the Force, use a webcam for this game. If your computer doesn't have a webcam, don't worry – you can use a mouse instead. If you're using a mouse, follow the boxed instruction in step 1 and then go straight to step 6.

1 Create a new project, then add this script to check that your webcam is working correctly. If you don't have a webcam, use the code below instead. This will enable you to control the game using the mouse.

```
when ⚑ clicked
turn video  on ▼
```

The TURN VIDEO ON block, located in the light-blue SENSING BLOCKS PALETTE, controls your computer's webcam.

No webcam?
Make this script instead so the training pod follows your mouse-pointer. Then go straight to step 6. You can also ignore the steps to adjust the webcam at the end of the project.

```
when ⚑ clicked
forever
    point towards  mouse-pointer ▼
    move 5 steps
```

2 Click the green flag [⚑] to run the new script. You should see a window pop up like this. Click "Allow" and you should see the view from your webcam on the STAGE behind the Cat sprite. Adjust the webcam so you can see yourself.

> Adobe Flash Player Settings.
>
> Camera and Microphone Access   **?**
>
> https://cdn.scratch.mit.edu is requesting access to your camera and microphone. If you click Allow you may be recorded.
>
> ✓ Allow   ⊖ Deny

3 As a test, follow these steps to create a script for using the webcam to move the cat around the STAGE. Go to the DATA BLOCKS PALETTE and make two new variables (for all sprites): "CutOff" and "SlowDown".

> Make a Variable
>
> ☐ **CutOff**
>
> ☐ **SlowDown**

Untick both boxes so the variables are not displayed on the STAGE.

"CutOff" and "SlowDown" are used to adjust how sensitive the sprite's movement is to the webcam.

This SENSING block has a value between 0 and 100 depending on how much you're moving in front of the webcam.

4 To enable the webcam to control the Cat sprite, add these blocks to the script you started in step one. The VIDEO ON STAGE blocks detect the movement, level and direction from the whole webcam picture. This information is used to move the cat across the STAGE. Make sure the windows in each of these blocks show the correct options.

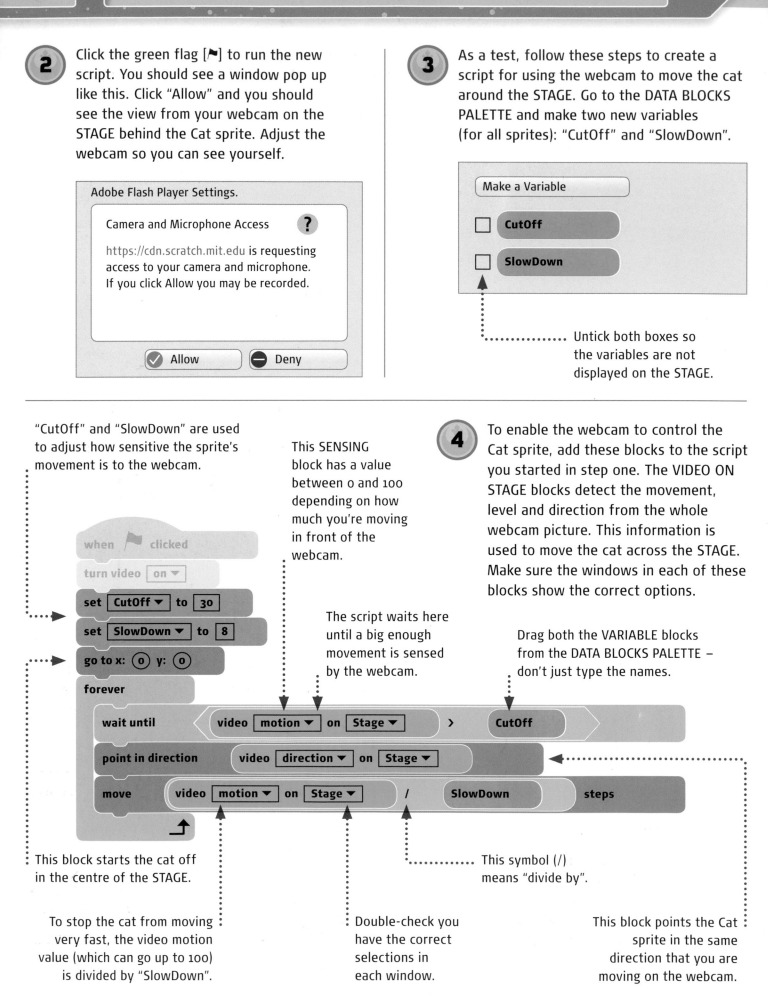

The script waits here until a big enough movement is sensed by the webcam.

Drag both the VARIABLE blocks from the DATA BLOCKS PALETTE – don't just type the names.

This block starts the cat off in the centre of the STAGE.

This symbol (/) means "divide by".

To stop the cat from moving very fast, the video motion value (which can go up to 100) is divided by "SlowDown".

Double-check you have the correct selections in each window.

This block points the Cat sprite in the same direction that you are moving on the webcam.

5 Control the cat by moving your hand around in front of the webcam. It might be easier if you look at the STAGE in full-screen mode. The cat should move in the same direction as any movement you make. As long as the cat is responding to your movement, it's fine to continue building the game – you'll see how to fine-tune the controls later on. If the cat isn't moving, check carefully that the code matches step 4 exactly.

6 Now it's time to replace the cat costume with a training pod. Click on the COSTUMES tab at the top of the screen and either click on the paintbrush to draw a new costume (see pages 14 to 15) or choose something suitable from the Scratch library. Rename the Cat sprite "Training Pod". Don't forget to centre your new sprite (see page 15).

New costume

Training Pod
Size: Approx. 75 x 75 pixels

Purpose: The training pod moves around to collect the crystals.

Collecting crystals

The player will practise controlling the Force by scooping up crystals. Scratch has a great way to make lots of working copies of a sprite: cloning. The code below makes cloned sprites for the player to collect.

7 Create a new sprite called "Blue Crystal". You can upload a picture to be your sprite or draw your own (see pages 14 to 15). Your crystal is best at about 45 x 45 pixels. Or, for now, you can use a sprite from the Scratch library, for example "Star1". It's easy to swap it for your own sprite later.

New sprite

Blue Crystal
Size: 45 x 45 pixels

Purpose: The player collects these crystals and scores a point for each one.

---

8 Each crystal will score one point, so click on the SCRIPTS tab, add a new variable called "Score" and select the option "For all sprites".

New Variable

Variable name: Score

● For all sprites   ○ For this sprite only

OK   Cancel

---

9 Add this new script to the Blue Crystal sprite to make ten cloned crystals on the STAGE. However, don't run the project yet, as the clones will be hidden until the next script is complete.

The score is reset to zero at the start of each game.

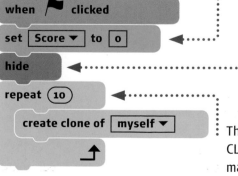

The original sprite is hidden. Only the clones are shown.

This loop runs the CREATE CLONE block 10 times to make 10 clones.

10 Scratch runs a special script for each clone when it's created. This script begins with a WHEN I START AS A CLONE block. Add this second script to the Blue Crystal sprite. Read through the script and see if you can work out what it tells each clone to do.

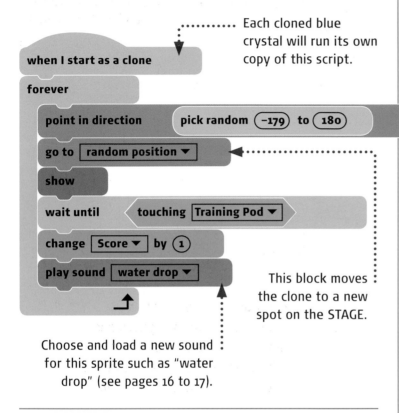

Each cloned blue crystal will run its own copy of this script.

when I start as a clone

forever

point in direction pick random (-179) to (180)

go to random position ▼

show

wait until touching Training Pod ▼

change Score ▼ by (1)

play sound water drop ▼

This block moves the clone to a new spot on the STAGE.

Choose and load a new sound for this sprite such as "water drop" (see pages 16 to 17).

11 Run the game. Ten blue crystals should appear on the STAGE. When the training pod touches a crystal, it should disappear as if it's been collected. The clone actually moves to a new position as if it's a new crystal appearing.

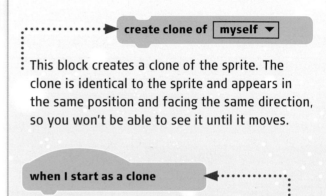

C-3PO says...

Clones

Clones in Scratch aren't humans grown on Kamino for the Clone Army; but, like clone soldiers, they are identical copies of an original. Clones are useful any time you want many copies of a sprite. In the CONTROL BLOCKS PALETTE, there are three yellow blocks that are used to control clones.

create clone of myself ▼

This block creates a clone of the sprite. The clone is identical to the sprite and appears in the same position and facing the same direction, so you won't be able to see it until it moves.

when I start as a clone

When a clone starts, it runs the script headed with this block. Clones don't run the sprite's main script, but they can run all other scripts in the sprite's SCRIPTS AREA, such as scripts triggered by messages.

delete this clone

This block gets rid of the clone. All clones disappear from the STAGE when a project stops, leaving just the original sprite.

Beware red crystals

To make things more interesting, there will be some unstable red crystals on the STAGE. Collect one of these sinister red gems by accident and you'll lose five points.

12 Create a new sprite for the red crystal (see pages 14 to 15). Click on either upload or paint at the top of the SPRITES LIST (this is a new sprite, not a costume). Your crystal is best at about 45 x 45 pixels. Or use something like the Star1 sprite from the Scratch library, but recolour it red using the fill tool in the paint editor.

New sprite

Red Crystal
Size: 45 x 45 pixels

Purpose: These red crystals are harmful. Each one loses the player five points when touched.

13 Give the Red Crystal sprite these two scripts. The first creates a new crystal every five seconds, and the second causes it to disappear when touched by the pod.

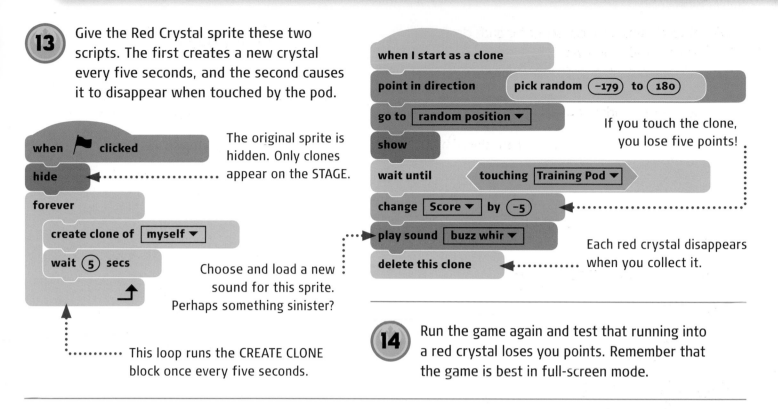

when 🏳 clicked
hide ◀········· The original sprite is hidden. Only clones appear on the STAGE.
forever
   create clone of [myself ▼]
   wait (5) secs

Choose and load a new sound for this sprite. Perhaps something sinister?

This loop runs the CREATE CLONE block once every five seconds.

when I start as a clone
point in direction [pick random (-179) to (180)]
go to [random position ▼]
show
wait until [touching [Training Pod ▼]]
change [Score ▼] by (-5)
play sound [buzz whir ▼]
delete this clone

If you touch the clone, you lose five points!

Each red crystal disappears when you collect it.

14 Run the game again and test that running into a red crystal loses you points. Remember that the game is best in full-screen mode.

Against the clock

At the moment, the game goes on forever! Add a 30-second countdown timer to put the player under pressure.

15 To add a countdown timer, first add a variable "Countdown" for all sprites and leave it showing on the STAGE. Then select the Training Pod sprite and add this script to end the game after 30 seconds.

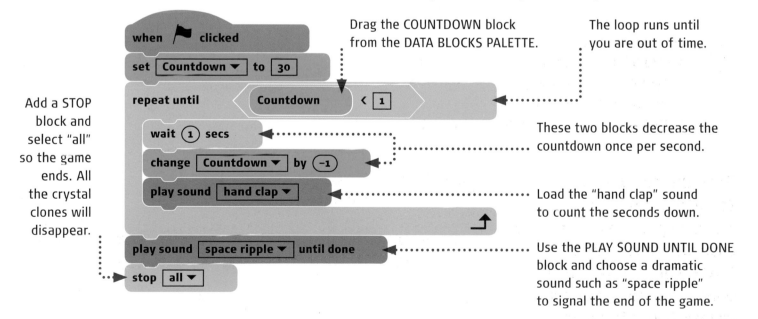

when 🏳 clicked
set [Countdown ▼] to (30)
repeat until < [Countdown] < [1] >
   wait (1) secs
   change [Countdown ▼] by (-1)
   play sound [hand clap ▼]
play sound [space ripple ▼] until done
stop [all ▼]

Add a STOP block and select "all" so the game ends. All the crystal clones will disappear.

Drag the COUNTDOWN block from the DATA BLOCKS PALETTE.

The loop runs until you are out of time.

These two blocks decrease the countdown once per second.

Load the "hand clap" sound to count the seconds down.

Use the PLAY SOUND UNTIL DONE block and choose a dramatic sound such as "space ripple" to signal the end of the game.

16 Run the game. When the countdown gets to zero, everything should stop with a dramatic noise and the crystals should disappear. How many points can you score? If you find the controls too sensitive or they're not responding, you can fine-tune the values of "SlowDown" and "CutOff" by following the instructions in the next section.

Fine-tuning

How responsive the training pod is to your movements on the webcam depends on the variables "CutOff" and "SlowDown" that you created right at the start of this project. This section shows you how to use sliders to find the best values.

 These blocks set the values of "CutOff" and "SlowDown".

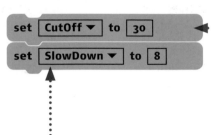

The training pod only moves when the motion value gets above this number. Increasing it stops the sprite from twitching at small movement values.

"SlowDown" adjusts the speed of the motion. The VIDEO MOTION block can have a value up to 100 so dividing by this number stops the pod from whizzing across the screen in a fraction of a second.

 In the DATA BLOCKS PALETTE, tick the boxes next to the CUTOFF block and the SLOWDOWN block so that the two variables are displayed on the STAGE.

Make a Variable

☑ **CutOff**

☑ **SlowDown**

.... Tick these boxes.

 You can play at different distances from the webcam. Use just a hand, your head or your whole body. It's easier to see what's going on if you use the full-screen mode. "SlowDown" will make the most difference to the controls. Right-click on the variable on the STAGE to change it into a slider to test different values easily.

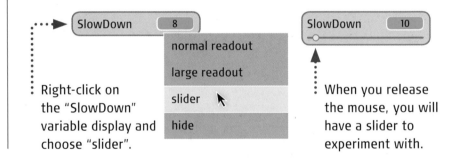

Right-click on the "SlowDown" variable display and choose "slider".

When you release the mouse, you will have a slider to experiment with.

 The slider changes the values and you can see the effect instantly. When you create a slider, you can select values between 0 and 100, which is too large a range to be useful here. Right-click again on the slider and choose "set slider min and max". Then enter "1" and "20" in the "Slider Range" box that appears.

Right-click here and select "set slider min and max".

Finally, click "OK" to set the range. ......

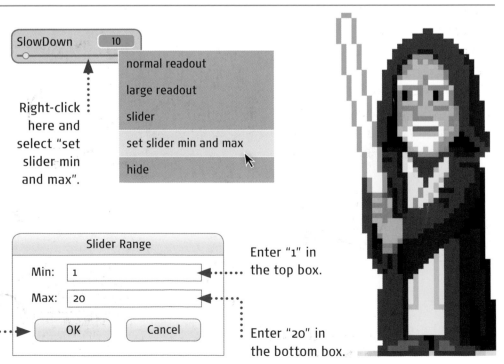

Enter "1" in the top box.

Enter "20" in the bottom box.

21 Now run the project and adjust the slider to see what value gives you the best control over the training pod.

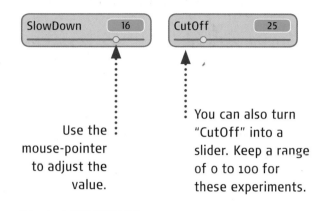

Use the mouse-pointer to adjust the value.

You can also turn "CutOff" into a slider. Keep a range of 0 to 100 for these experiments.

22 Once you're happy with the numbers, copy them into the SET TO blocks at the top of the script. This stops the game from resetting to the old values when you rerun the game. To stop the variables from showing on the STAGE, go to the DATA BLOCKS PALETTE and untick the boxes next to each variable.

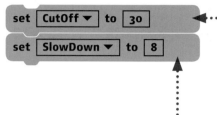

Put your best value from your "CutOff" slider in here.

Put your best value from your "SlowDown" slider in here.

Now try this!

The instructions here are just a starting point. Once you've got the game working, you can make it your own by diving into the code and experimenting. It's very easy to copy scripts you've already got to use with new sprites.

Too easy? Too hard?

You can experiment with other aspects of the game to adjust the difficulty level. Have a look at the crystals' code. Can you work out how to create a different number of crystal clones? Or how to change the delay before each red crystal appears? It's also easy to adjust the sizes of the training pod or the crystals by adding a SET SIZE block to any sprite. Adjust the size and rerun the game to see what impact it has.

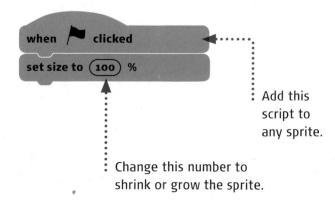

Add this script to any sprite.

Change this number to shrink or grow the sprite.

C-3PO says...

Ideas to recycle

Look back at the extra ideas at the end of the Cargo Bay Chase (see pages 32 and 33). You can use the same ideas in this game.

➤ See how to save a copy of your game so you can experiment without fear of losing anything.

➤ Can you adapt the high-score code to work in this game?

➤ Choose some music and add a script to play it in a loop.

More unusual controls

This game introduced a fun new way to control sprites in Scratch. Can you think of any other games that would work with webcam controls? There is also a LOUDNESS block in the SENSING BLOCKS PALETTE that uses your computer's microphone to sense sound. Can you make a game controlled by shouting?

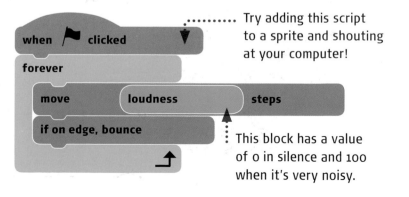

Try adding this script to a sprite and shouting at your computer!

This block has a value of 0 in silence and 100 when it's very noisy.

Secret Spy Mission

How would you fare on a mission into enemy territory to gather secret intelligence? Now is your chance to join the ranks of brave, plucky droids like BB-8 and R2-D2, and go on a perilous assignment. Can you outwit the patrolling soldiers and gather vital information stored on datacards?

Aim of the game

Use the arrow keys to steer your droid around the enemy base to collect datacards. The patrolling soldiers might be faster than the droid, but the droid is far more cunning. It has hacked into the data network and found a way to get advance warning of the soldiers' patrols so a countdown tells you when the soldiers will next turn around.

**Breep Broo.
Breeee-Worp!
Wrrrp Breeep Broo!**

The timer shows how much time is left before the soldiers turn around and reverse their patrols.

Secret Spy Mission
by CleverLittleDroid (unshared)

5

The droid is moved using the arrow keys.

Walls form a maze and can't be walked through.

How to build the game

Secret Spy Mission relies on the sensing of collisions between objects. In order to make this work well, it's best to start with a ball sprite from the Scratch library to represent the droid. You can add a separate droid sprite later that follows the movements of this simpler sprite.

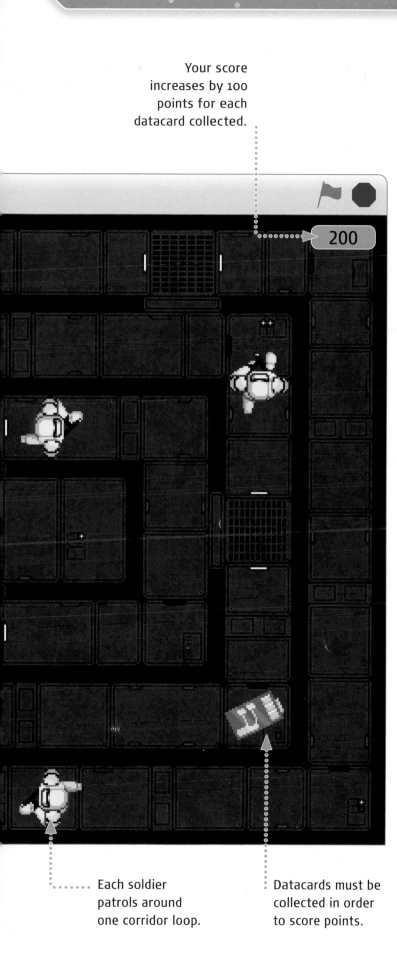

Your score increases by 100 points for each datacard collected.

200

Each soldier patrols around one corridor loop.

Datacards must be collected in order to score points.

1 Create a new project and delete the Cat sprite. Click on the library button [♠] in the NEW SPRITE menu and load the sprite named "Ball". Click on the blue "i" icon, rename the sprite "Player" and then press the blue arrow to go back.

Player

2 Click on the DATA BLOCKS PALETTE and create a variable called "playerSpeed". Make sure you select "For this sprite only" and untick the box next to the variable on the BLOCKS PALETTE so it doesn't appear on the STAGE.

New Variable
Variable name: playerSpeed
○ For all sprites   ● For this sprite only ◀
OK   Cancel

Make sure you choose this option.

3 Add this script to the Player sprite. It makes the sprite move up the screen when the up arrow key is pressed.

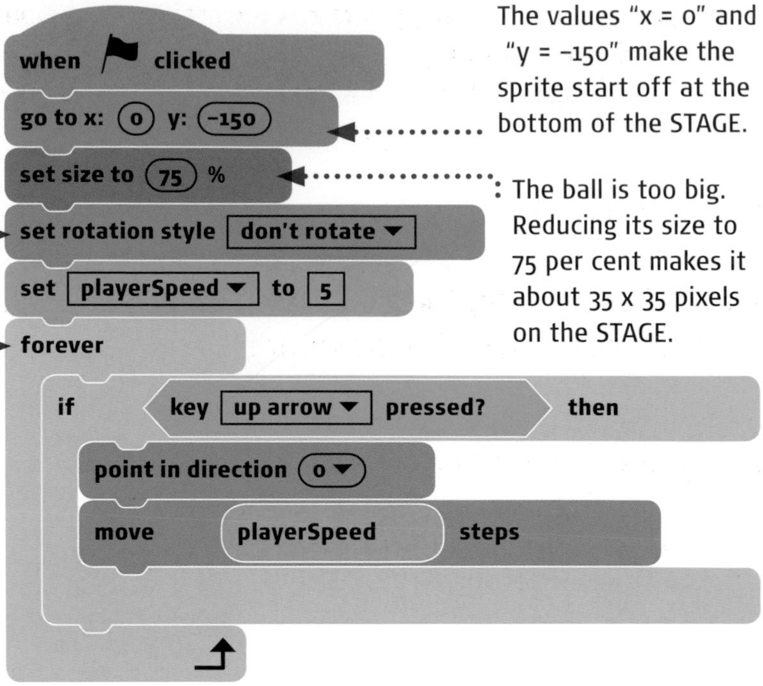
when [flag] clicked
go to x: 0 y: –150
set size to 75 %
set rotation style don't rotate
set playerSpeed to 5
forever
if key up arrow pressed? then
point in direction 0
move playerSpeed steps

The values "x = 0" and "y = –150" make the sprite start off at the bottom of the STAGE.

The ball is too big. Reducing its size to 75 per cent makes it about 35 x 35 pixels on the STAGE.

Set this option carefully; it's important later when sensing collisions with the base walls.

This script inside the FOREVER loop checks on the up arrow key over and over. If it's pressed then the sprite moves 10 steps upwards.

4 Click the green flag [⚑] to run the project. You should be able to make the ball rise up the STAGE using the up arrow key.

5 To make the Player sprite move in all the directions of the arrow keys, add three more blocks inside the FOREVER loop. Each IF-THEN block senses a different key, turns the sprite in the correct direction and then moves it five steps.

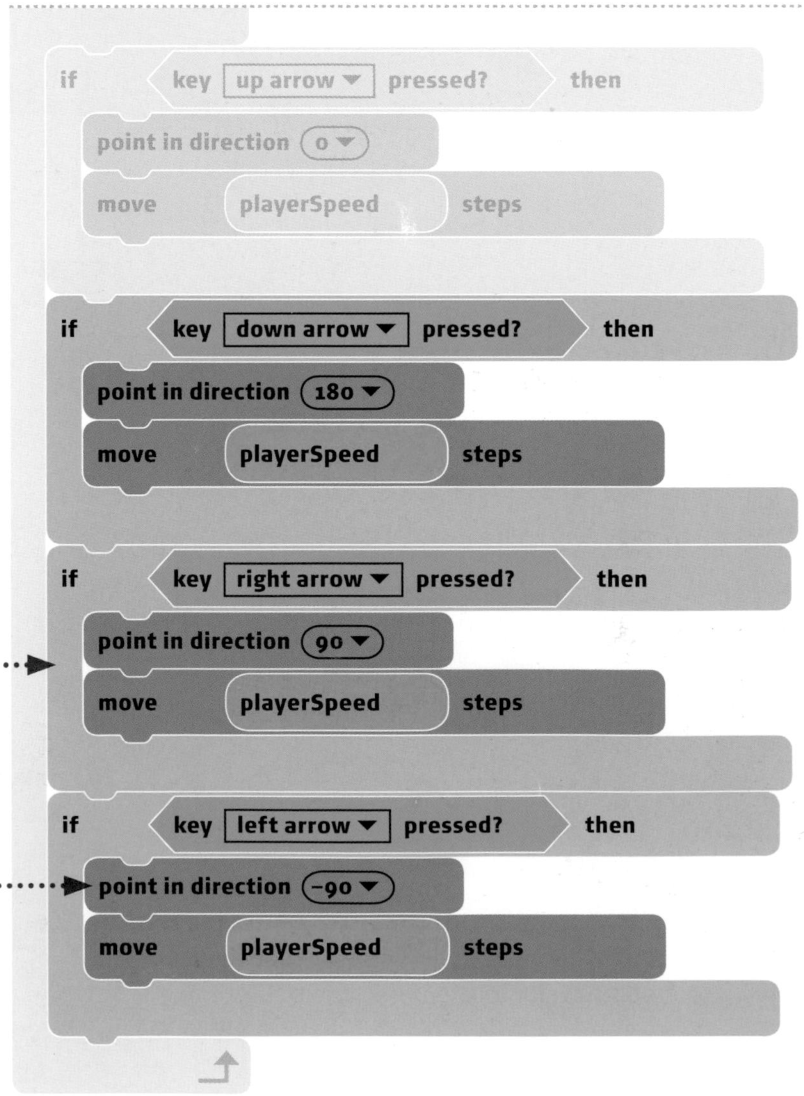
if key up arrow pressed? then
point in direction 0
move playerSpeed steps
if key down arrow pressed? then
point in direction 180
move playerSpeed steps
if key right arrow pressed? then
point in direction 90
move playerSpeed steps
if key left arrow pressed? then
point in direction –90
move playerSpeed steps

Each IF-THEN block should be inside the FOREVER loop, but not inside any of the other IF-THEN blocks.

Make sure the direction value chosen matches the arrow key.

6 Click on the green flag [] to run the project. You should be able to move the yellow ball using the arrow keys. If there are any problems, check your script very carefully.

Adding a droid

Now it's time to add a sprite to act as the decoration for the Player sprite. While the Player sprite does all the hard work sensing collisions, this new Droid sprite just looks the part.

7 Click on the paintbrush icon [/] in the NEW SPRITE menu, above the SPRITES LIST. Draw your droid from above and facing to the right (see pages 14 to 15). Centre the sprite accurately or it won't turn properly. Click on the blue "i" icon to name your sprite "Droid".

New sprite

Droid

Size: Approx. 35 x 35 pixels

Purpose: Travels the STAGE collecting datacards and outwitting enemy soldiers.

8 Now make the Droid sprite stick to the Player sprite like glue and point in the same direction that the player is moving. Select the Droid sprite and click on the SCRIPTS tab. Add this script to the droid. Read the script carefully to see what it does.

You'll find this block with the light-blue SENSING blocks.

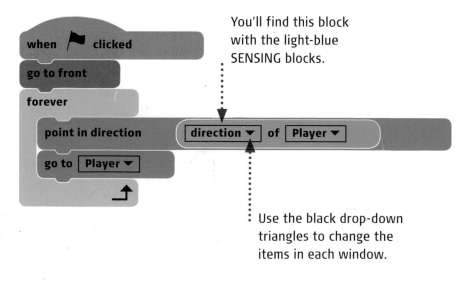

```
when [flag] clicked
go to front
forever
    point in direction [direction ▼] of [Player ▼]
    go to [Player ▼]
```

Use the black drop-down triangles to change the items in each window.

9 Run the project and you should be able to drive your Droid sprite around using the arrow keys. If you can see the Ball costume beneath it, don't worry – it will be made invisible later on.

Move along... move along.

Collecting data

Your droid is on a mission to collect datacards from around the enemy base. This section adds the code to make the Datacard sprite appear in random locations.

New sprite

Datacard

Size: Approx. 40 x 40 pixels

Purpose: Datacards appear at random for the droid to collect for 100 points each.

10   Click on the paintbrush icon [/] in the NEW SPRITE menu, above the SPRITES LIST. Draw your new sprite and call it "Datacard".

11   Click on the SCRIPTS tab, add a variable called "Score" and select "For all sprites". Keep it showing on the STAGE. On the STAGE, right-click on the "Score" window and select "large readout" so the name disappears. Drag the new score display to the top-right corner of the STAGE.

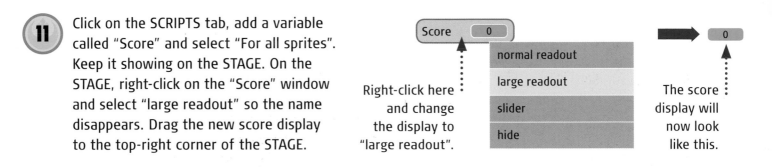

Right-click here and change the display to "large readout".

| normal readout |
| large readout |
| slider |
| hide |

The score display will now look like this.

12   To make datacards appear, add this script to the sprite. Read through the script to ensure you understand what's going on. The script spends most of the time waiting for the Player sprite to touch the datacard.

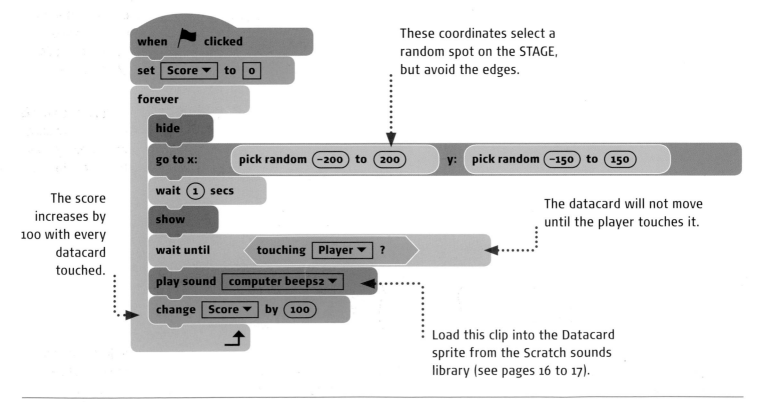

These coordinates select a random spot on the STAGE, but avoid the edges.

The score increases by 100 with every datacard touched.

The datacard will not move until the player touches it.

Load this clip into the Datacard sprite from the Scratch sounds library (see pages 16 to 17).

13   Run the game and score some points by steering the droid around to collect the datacards. Your score should rise and the datacard should appear in a new location each time you touch it.

Time for some walls

The enemy base is a dangerous place full of narrow corridors. In this section you'll see how to draw the base's walls, which make the game interesting.

 14 Add a new sprite using the paintbrush icon [/] in the NEW SPRITE menu. The paint editor will appear. Click on the blue "i" icon to name your sprite "Base".

New sprite

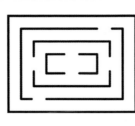

Base
Size: Approx. 480 x 360 pixels

Purpose: Forms the background of the game, including the obstacles that the droid must steer around.

 15 In the paint editor, make sure "Bitmap Mode" is selected in the bottom-right corner. If it isn't, click the "Convert to bitmap" button to change the mode. Also make sure that the zoom at the bottom right reads 100 per cent so you're drawing the size of the whole STAGE. Choose the line tool and set the line width control to the middle. Then pick a dark colour for the walls.

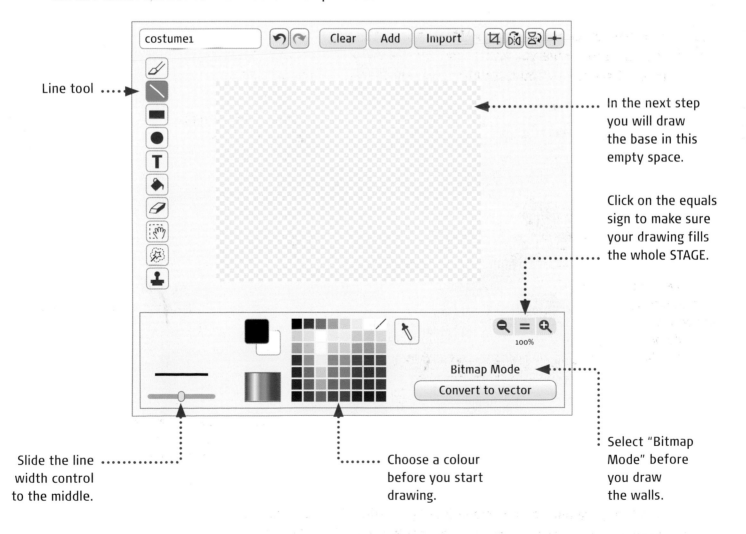

Line tool

In the next step you will draw the base in this empty space.

Click on the equals sign to make sure your drawing fills the whole STAGE.

Bitmap Mode
Convert to vector

Slide the line width control to the middle.

Choose a colour before you start drawing.

Select "Bitmap Mode" before you draw the walls.

16 Now draw the walls. Start by drawing the outside wall at the outer edge of the chequered drawing area. Hold down the Shift key on your keyboard to make sure lines are perfectly vertical or horizontal. Then add the inside walls.

Don't try to set the centre: It will delete parts of your sprite!

Hold Shift as you draw with the line tool for perfectly horizontal or vertical lines.

Copy this pattern. It gives four loops for the soldiers to patrol.

Eraser tool

The outer wall must be complete, with no gaps.

Selection tool

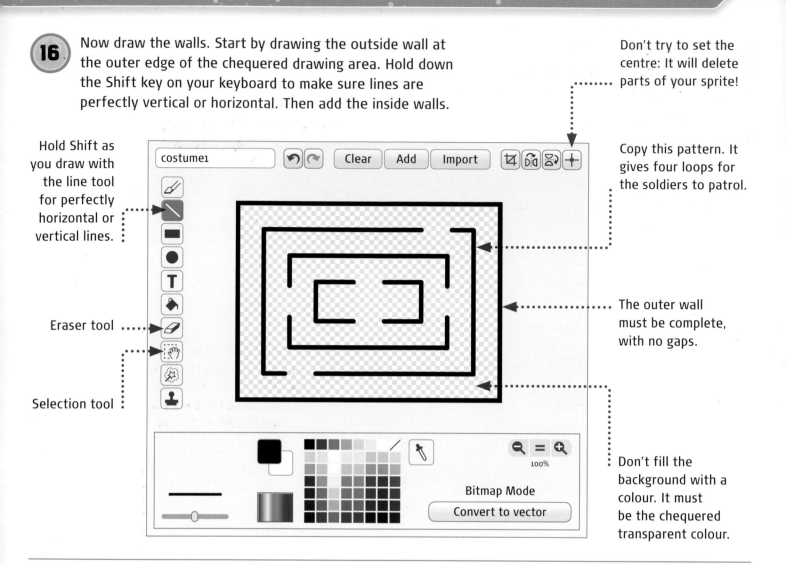

costume1   Clear   Add   Import   100%   Bitmap Mode   Convert to vector

Don't fill the background with a colour. It must be the chequered transparent colour.

17 To make your base appear centred on the STAGE, click on the SCRIPTS tab and add this script to the Base sprite. Run the project and you'll see your base design in the middle of the STAGE.

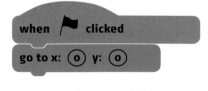

when 🏳 clicked
go to x: ⓞ y: ⓞ

18 You might need to fine-tune your base costume to make sure the droid can fit through all the passages. To alter the walls, select the Base sprite and click the COSTUMES tab. Use the eraser tool to remove walls and the selection tool to move them.

19 If you use the eraser, be careful not to leave any stray paint spots behind as the droid will stop if it hits them. Check the corners of the base for bumps that the player might get stuck on and remove them.

Passages should be wide enough for the droid to travel through.

Remove any bumps with the eraser tool.

Stop the droid from cheating

At the moment the player can walk through the walls of the soldiers' base. Adding more code will stop the plucky droid from ignoring the laws of physics.

 20 Select the Player sprite and add this code into the main script in four places so the walls block the droid's path. These blocks will reverse any movement that ends with the sprite overlapping a wall.

This block exactly reverses the move just made. The minus sign (–) makes the sprite take backwards steps. ....▶

The new blocks go inside each IF-THEN block, after the MOVE block. There is a new IF-THEN block for each of the four directions.

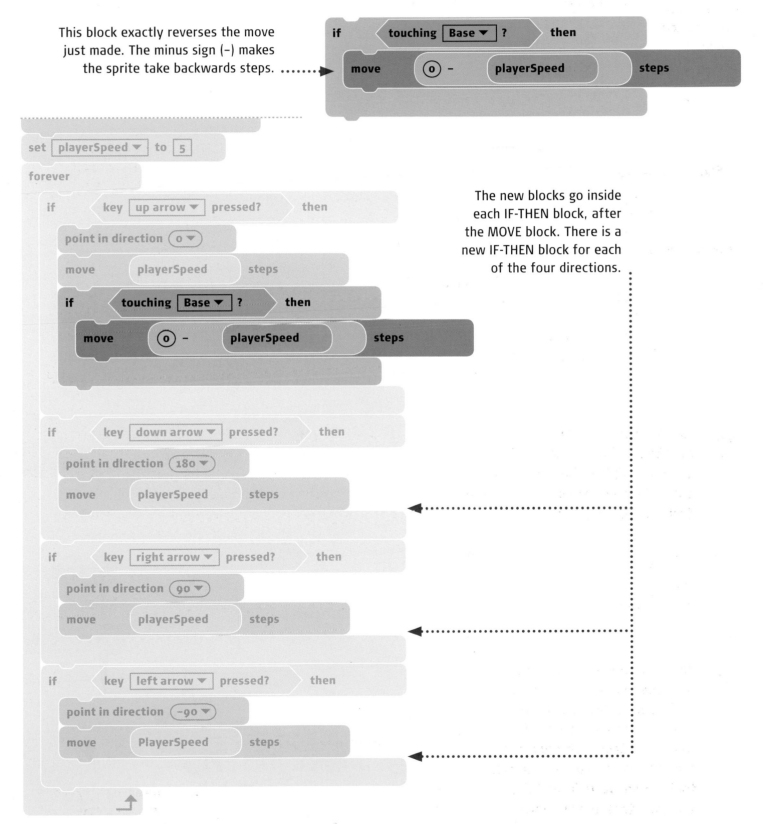

How does it work?

You might wonder why the droid has to move five steps backwards. The reason is that it normally moves forwards five steps at a time. The backward move reverses the forward one, making the droid stand still. This happens so quickly that you don't see it move.

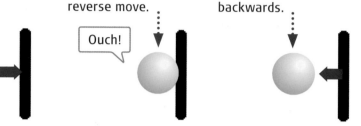

The player moves five steps forwards.

Touching the wall triggers the reverse move.

The player moves five steps backwards.

Ouch!

21 Adjust the droid's starting point by changing the x and y values in the GO TO block at the start of the player's script. A spot in the top left-hand corner of the STAGE works well. You can drag the Player sprite into position, then copy its coordinates into the GO TO block.

Use the coordinates that appear in the top-right corner of the SCRIPTS AREA. ......

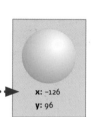

x: –126
y: 96

Copy the x and y values into this block at the beginning of your script.

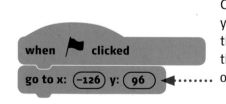

when 🏳 clicked
go to x: (–126) y: (96) ◄ ·······

22 Try the game. Check the droid can get down every passage without getting stuck. If it can't, you might need to move the walls in the Base sprite or shrink the Player sprite a little. Check the droid can't walk through the walls. If it can, carefully check the script changes from step 20. If the Player sprite refuses to move, check that the background of the Base sprite is the chequered transparent colour.

Here come the soldiers

At the moment, it's not hard to collect the datacards. Follow these steps to add some enemies so the droid has to move around more tactically.

23 As with the droid, it's best to start with a plain sprite and add a soldier appearance later. Load the "Ball" sprite from the library []. Open the COSTUMES tab and select the blue costume. Rename the sprite "Enemy1".

Enemy1

C-3PO says...

If-then-else
The IF-THEN-ELSE block is like an IF-THEN block, but with an extra trick. IF-THEN asks a question and runs the blocks inside only if the answer is yes. IF-THEN-ELSE holds two groups of blocks: one to run if the answer is yes, and another for if the answer is no.

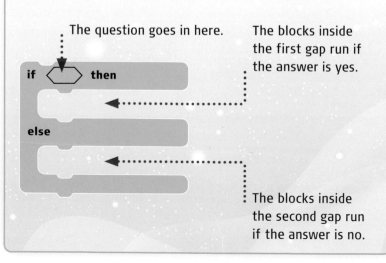

The question goes in here.

if ⬡ then

else

The blocks inside the first gap run if the answer is yes.

The blocks inside the second gap run if the answer is no.

24 Make sure the Enemy1 sprite is selected, click on the SCRIPTS tab and create two new variables ("for this sprite only") called "enSpeed" and "reversed". Untick them so that they don't show on the STAGE. Add this new script to the Enemy1 sprite to make the enemy patrol in a rectangular pattern and to stop the game if the Enemy1 and Player sprites come into contact.

This value sets the enemy's speed.

Set this option carefully: It's important later when sensing collisions with the base walls.

This variable controls whether the enemy patrols clockwise (0) or anticlockwise (1).

This sets the enemy's starting point.

This part of the script stops the enemy from walking through walls by making it turn when it touches one.

The MINUS block inside this MOVE block makes it the reverse of the last move.

Use an IF-THEN-ELSE block here, not just an IF-THEN block. It turns the enemy right or left depending on the value of "reversed".

This IF-THEN block stops the game if the player is caught. Make sure it's after the IF-THEN block above, not inside it.

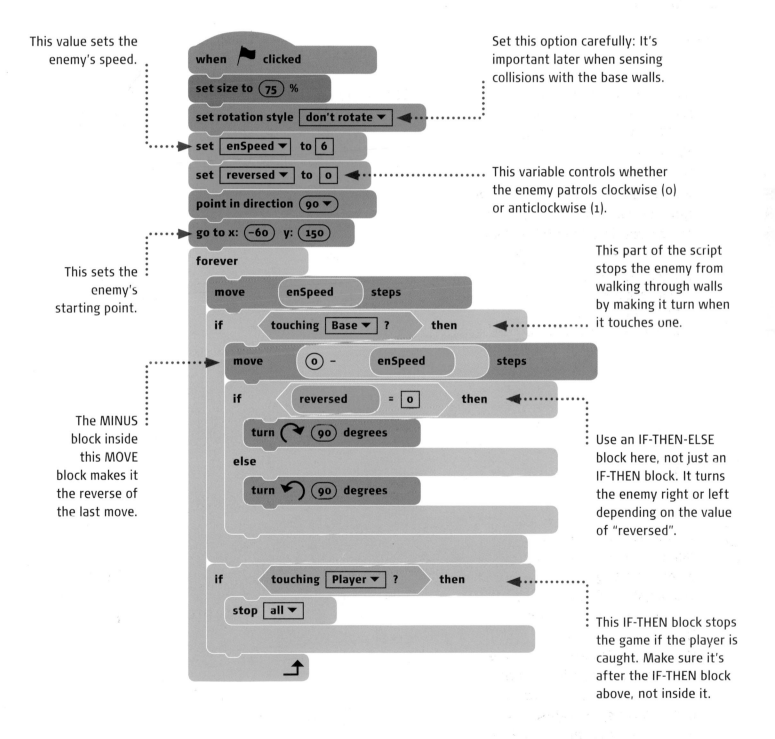

C-3PO says...

Messages

Sending messages is a useful way to pass secret intelligence to rebel fighters. However, in Scratch messages are used to tell sprites to do something. When a message is sent out using a BROADCAST block, every script that has a matching header will run.

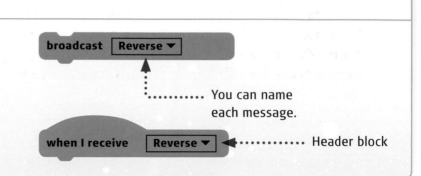

You can name each message.

Header block

 25

The game will broadcast a message to tell the Enemy sprite to reverse its patrols. This message doesn't exist yet, so you need to add it to the list of Scratch messages. To do this, add a WHEN I RECEIVE MESSAGE1 block to the SCRIPTS AREA. Select "new message" using the drop-down menu. Name your message "Reverse".

Click on the triangle to see the menu and select "new message".

Type "Reverse" here. Then click "OK".

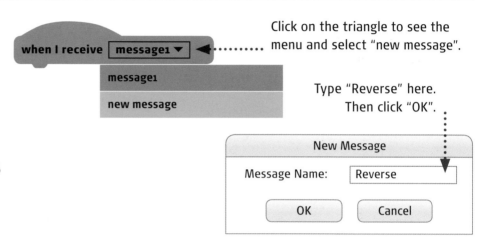

New Message

Message Name: Reverse

OK   Cancel

 26

Under the new header block, add these blocks to change the direction of Enemy1 when it receives the "Reverse" message. In step 29, you'll add a script to send that message every 15 seconds.

The value of the variable is reversed here (0 swaps to 1 and vice versa). This turns the sprite in the opposite direction when it touches the walls.

This is the block you just added.

This block reverses the soldier's direction of travel.

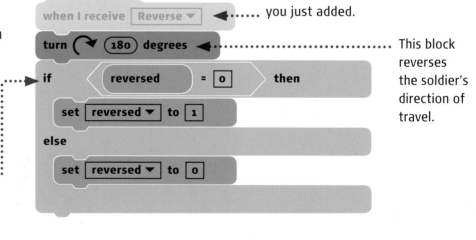

 27

Run the game. The blue ball should patrol all the way around the loop. If it starts on a wall, tweak the x and y coordinates at the start of its script so it starts in a clear space.

28

To make the soldier reverse its patrol, you need a script that sends the "Reverse" message every 15 seconds. Create a new sprite by clicking the paintbrush icon [✏] in the NEW SPRITE menu, and name it "Timer". It doesn't need a costume as it doesn't appear on the STAGE. It's only used as a timer for broadcasting the message "Reverse".

29 Click on the SCRIPTS tab and add a new variable called "ReverseTimer" for all sprites. Show this variable on the STAGE, right-click on it and select "large readout". Drag it to a place on the STAGE where it won't get in the way of the action. Add this script to the empty Timer sprite, but be careful which blocks go inside other blocks or it won't work. Every 15 seconds this script sends the message to make the enemy reverse.

when ⚑ clicked

forever

> set ReverseTimer ▼ to 15
>
> repeat until ⟨ ReverseTimer = 0 ⟩
>
> > wait 1 secs
> >
> > change ReverseTimer ▼ by -1
> >
> > if ⟨ ReverseTimer < 5 ⟩ then
> >
> > > play sound pop ▼
>
> broadcast Reverse ▼
>
> wait 1 secs

The IF-THEN block makes a "pop" sound for the last 5 seconds.

This BROADCAST block triggers Enemy1's reversing script (see step 26).

30 Run the game. The Enemy1 sprite should patrol around the outer corridor. Every 15 seconds it will turn around and patrol in the opposite direction.

31 It's time to show the soldier properly. Create a new sprite and draw your soldier from above and facing to the right.

New sprite

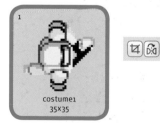

Soldier

Size: Approx. 35 x 35 pixels

Purpose: These soldiers patrol the base. If the player runs into them, it's game over.

32 If you want to make your soldier appear to walk, you can animate the sprite. Select the COSTUMES tab and right-click on "costume1". Make a duplicate, then use the flip up-down tool to make a mirror image.

costume1
35×35

costume2
35×35

The flip up-down tool

33 Click on the SCRIPTS tab and add this new script to make your Soldier sprite follow Enemy1's position and direction.

34 If you made more than one costume to animate the Soldier sprite, add this new script to swap the costumes as the sprite moves.

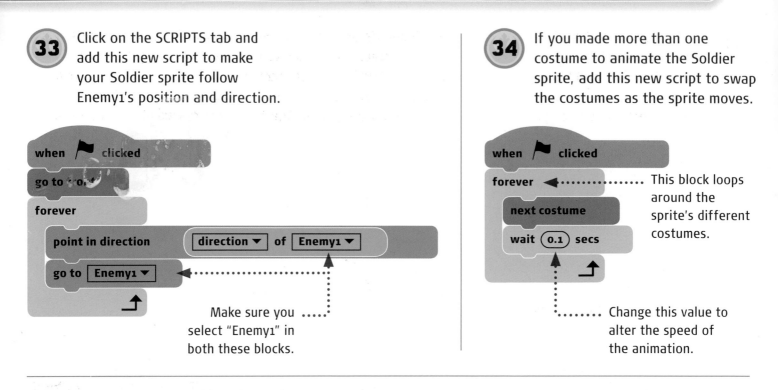

Make sure you select "Enemy1" in both these blocks.

This block loops around the sprite's different costumes.

Change this value to alter the speed of the animation.

35 Run the game. Your soldier should move in a large square around the outer corridor. Every 15 seconds it will reverse the direction of its patrol.

More soldiers

To make life even more dangerous for the droid, you can have four soldiers patrolling the base. Just follow these steps.

37 Go into Enemy2. Change its starting x and y positions, direction and reversed values to the numbers below. Now it will it patrol the second loop, in the opposite direction to Enemy1. If the sprite appears on top of a wall, adjust its x and y coordinates.

36 Right-click on the Enemy1 sprite and select "duplicate". A new sprite named "Enemy2" will appear in the SPRITES LIST. Do this twice more so you have four sprites called "Enemy1", "Enemy2", "Enemy3" and "Enemy4".

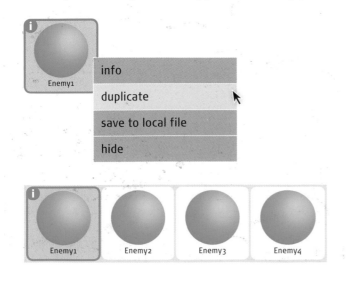

This value controls which way the enemy turns at each wall.

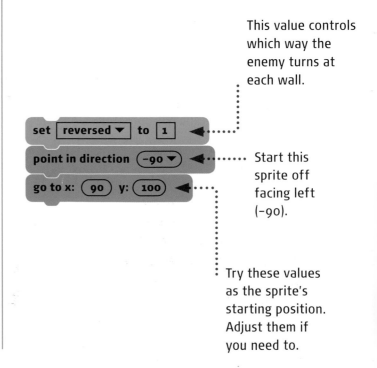

Start this sprite off facing left (-90).

Try these values as the sprite's starting position. Adjust them if you need to.

38 Go into Enemy3. Adjust the x and y coordinates only. It will patrol the third loop from the outer edge, in the same direction as Enemy1.

go to x: (60) y: (55)

39 Enemy4 will patrol in the centre. Change its x and y coordinates and reversed values as below so that it moves in the same direction as Enemy2. Adjust x and y until Enemy4 isn't touching a wall. Also, slow its speed right down so the player has a chance of getting in and out of the central area.

Change this sprite's speed to "3". ....

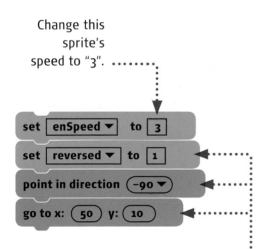

set enSpeed ▼ to 3

set reversed ▼ to 1 ◀ · · · · · · · ·

point in direction (-90 ▼) ◀ · · · · · ·

go to x: (50) y: (10) ◀ · · · · · · · · ·

Experiment with these values.

40 Run the game. Make sure all four sprites make it all the way around their patrol. You might need to adjust the walls a little or shrink the enemy sprite. The game should stop if an enemy touches the player.

41 Now it's time to make extra copies of the Soldier sprite. Duplicate the soldier sprite three times to get "Soldier2", "Soldier3" and "Soldier4". Alter each soldier sprite's script to follow the correct enemy sprite: Soldier2 follows Enemy2 and so on. Run the game and watch them patrol.

Adjust "Enemy2" to the correct soldier sprite in both places.

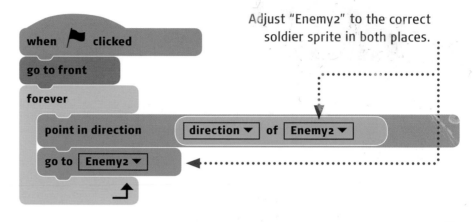

when ⚑ clicked

go to front

forever

point in direction   direction ▼ of Enemy2 ▼

go to Enemy2 ▼   ◀ · · · · · · ·

42 To neaten things up, use a SET GHOST EFFECT block to make all the ball sprites invisible. A HIDE block won't work for this, since hidden sprites can't sense when they're touching other sprites, whereas ghosted sprites can. Add this short script to each of the Player, Enemy1, Enemy2, Enemy3 and Enemy4 sprites.

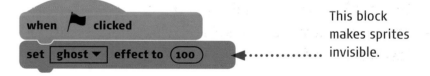

when ⚑ clicked

set ghost ▼ effect to (100) ◀ · · · · · · · · · ·

This block makes sprites invisible.

43 Run the game. You should now just see the droid and the four soldier sprites, and no yellow or blue balls. You can now play the game. Challenge your friends to set a high score!

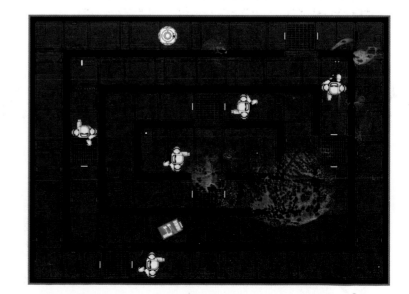

Asteroid Dash

Do you think you could pilot your way through an asteroid field as well as Han Solo and Chewbacca? This game lets you try. Follow the steps to build the game, then challenge your friends to beat your score. Who can fly the most parsecs?

Aim of the game

Steer your way through a hazardous sector of space for as long as you can, while dodging asteroids and laser-firing enemy ships. The left and right arrow keys sweep your space freighter around the STAGE. If things get too dangerous, you can trigger the ship's hyperdrive by pressing the up arrow, but beware: It takes a while to recharge.

You've never heard of the *Millennium Falcon*? It's the ship that made the Kessel Run in less than 12 parsecs!

How many parsecs can you travel before your ship is destroyed? Your parsec meter acts as your score.

Asteroid Dash
by FlyboyAce (unshared)

Parsecs   0.386

Stars whizz past as you play.

Enemy ships spiral across the screen firing lasers at you. To survive, don't crash into them and dodge their laser blasts.

Steer clear of the tumbling asteroids. Collide with one, and your ship will explode!

Asteroids do not concern me, Admiral. I want that ship!

You control your spaceship using the left and right arrow keys.

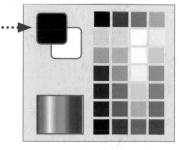

How to build the game
To give the illusion of flying through space, stars will whizz past the player. The first task is to make this simulation. Each flying star is a clone – a fully working, independent copy of a single sprite.

1 Start a new project and call it "Asteroid Dash". Right-click on the Cat sprite and select "Delete". To create a space-like backdrop, click on the paintbrush icon [✏] in the NEW BACKDROP menu in the STAGE INFO area. Use the fill tool [🪣] to turn the backdrop black.

First choose black on the palette.

Next select the fill tool [🪣] and click on the backdrop to make it black. ....➤

2 The Star sprite is just a tiny white spot. To make it, click on the paintbrush icon [/] in the NEW SPRITE menu, above the SPRITES LIST. The paint editor will open. Follow the numbered steps on the diagram below in order to draw the small white square. The first step is to zoom in to 1,600 per cent so you can see what you're doing clearly.

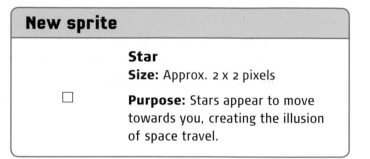

New sprite

☐ **Star**
Size: Approx. 2 x 2 pixels

Purpose: Stars appear to move towards you, creating the illusion of space travel.

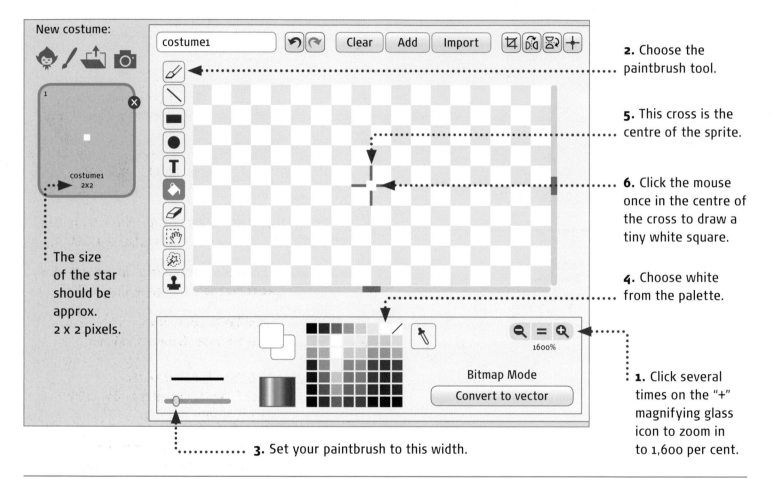

New costume:

costume1

Clear   Add   Import

1600%

Bitmap Mode
Convert to vector

The size of the star should be approx. 2 x 2 pixels.

2. Choose the paintbrush tool.

5. This cross is the centre of the sprite.

6. Click the mouse once in the centre of the cross to draw a tiny white square.

4. Choose white from the palette.

1. Click several times on the "+" magnifying glass icon to zoom in to 1,600 per cent.

3. Set your paintbrush to this width.

---

3 Under the SCRIPTS tab, select the DATA heading and click "Make a Variable". Call the variable "starSpeed" and select "For this sprite only", so that each clone can have its own speed value. Click "OK", then untick the variable's box so it doesn't show on the STAGE.

This option allows each clone to have its own speed.

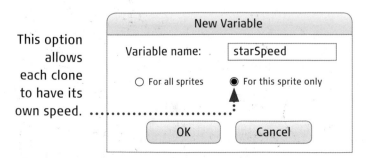

New Variable

Variable name: starSpeed

○ For all sprites   ● For this sprite only

OK   Cancel

4 Make another variable, "Hyperdrive", for all sprites. Untick its box so it doesn't show on the STAGE. The value of "Hyperdrive" is set to 1 when your ship goes to lightspeed, and it makes stars show trails. The code to trigger this effect will be added in step 13.

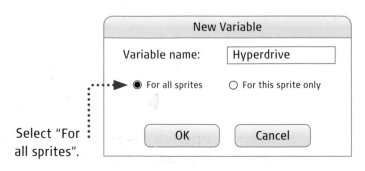

New Variable

Variable name: Hyperdrive

● For all sprites   ○ For this sprite only

OK   Cancel

Select "For all sprites".

5 Now add these two scripts to the Star sprite. The first script makes new cloned stars at random. The second script makes each clone fly out from the centre of the STAGE to the edge, then vanish.

when ⚑ clicked

hide

go to x: ⓪ y: ⓪

forever

    if ⟨ pick random ① to ③ = 1 ⟩ then

        create clone of [myself ▼]

Only the clones are visible, not the original Star sprite.

Each star starts at the centre of the STAGE.

New clones are given a random direction and speed.

Clones are created 1 out of every 3 times the loop runs.

when I start as a clone

point in direction   pick random (−179) to (180)

set [starSpeed ▼] to   pick random ② to ⑩

set size to   (20) * [starSpeed] %

show

repeat until ⟨ touching [edge ▼] ? ⟩

    move [starSpeed] steps

    if ⟨ [Hyperdrive] = 1 ⟩ then

        stamp

delete this clone

The faster stars are nearer, so the MULTIPLY (*) block makes them slightly bigger.

Drag the STARSPEED and the HYPERDRIVE blocks from the DATA BLOCKS PALETTE.

This loop moves the star clones out from the centre to the edge of the STAGE.

The IF-THEN block leaves star trails when the hyperdrive effect is on.

The STAMP block (from the PEN BLOCKS PALETTE) copies an image of the sprite onto the STAGE.

The star clones disappear when they reach the edge of the STAGE.

6 To test your new code, click on the green flag [⚑] and run the project. Stars should fly out from the centre of the STAGE as if you're flying through space. It will look best in full-screen mode.

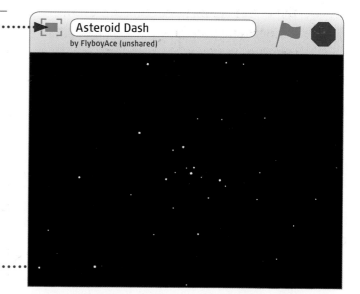

Click here to make the project fill the screen.

Notice how the stars disappear when they reach the edge of the STAGE.

Add an asteroid field

The asteroids work just like the stars: A single Asteroid sprite is cloned, and the clones are shown moving from the centre of the STAGE to the edge. When you pilot the spaceship – which you'll add in step 12 – you'll need to avoid the asteroids to stay in the game.

C-3PO says...

Stamps
The STAMP block leaves an image of the sprite on the STAGE at its current position. It's not a clone, just a snapshot of the sprite.

7 To draw your Asteroid sprite, click on the paintbrush icon [/] in the NEW SPRITES menu, above the SPRITES LIST. Reset the zoom to 100 per cent. Name your new sprite "Asteroid". You can make it a simple shape like a circle to get the game working, then redraw a more detailed costume for the asteroid later.

New sprite

Asteroid
Size: Approx. 90 x 90 pixels

Purpose: Asteroids hurtle through space. If you collide with one, it's game over.

8 Now click on the SCRIPTS tab and build the script shown on the right. It will make the Asteroid sprite spawn a new asteroid with a probability of 1 in 30 – that's 10 times less likely than each new star.

Only the clones will be visible.

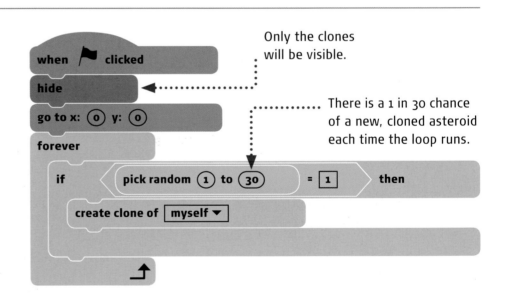

There is a 1 in 30 chance of a new, cloned asteroid each time the loop runs.

9 Just like the stars, each asteroid will move at its own speed. Select DATA in the BLOCKS PALETTE and click on "Make a Variable". Call the variable "astSpeed" (short for "asteroid speed") and select "For this sprite only", so that each clone can have its own, separate speed value. Click "OK" to make the variable, then untick its box so it doesn't show on the STAGE.

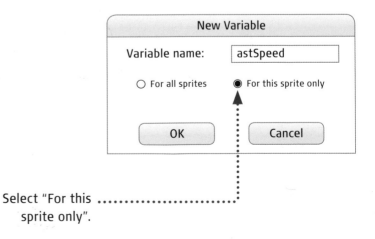

Select "For this sprite only".

10 Next add this script to the Asteroid sprite. It will be run by each new asteroid clone. The clones will appear at the centre of the STAGE, then get larger as they move towards the edge.

Asteroids start off looking small because they are far away.

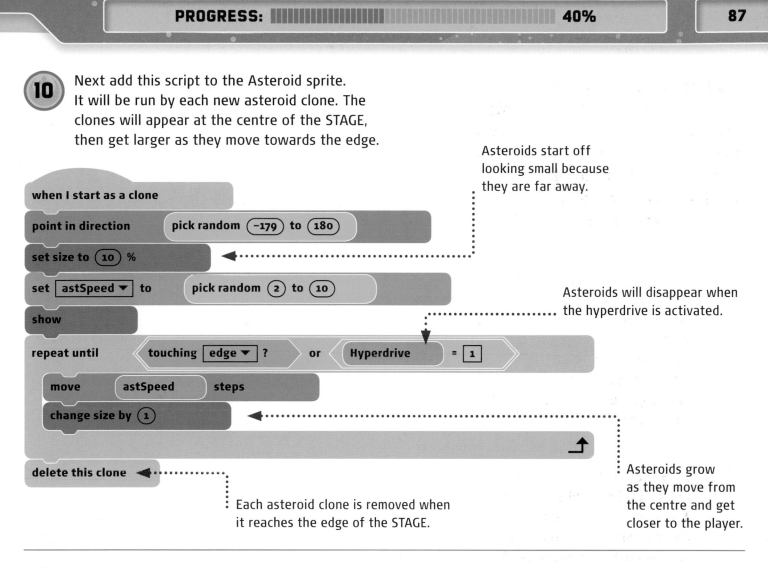

```
when I start as a clone
point in direction    pick random (-179) to (180)
set size to (10) %
set astSpeed ▼ to    pick random (2) to (10)
show
repeat until    < touching edge ▼ ? >  or  < Hyperdrive = [1] >
    move    astSpeed    steps
    change size by (1)

delete this clone
```

Asteroids will disappear when the hyperdrive is activated.

Asteroids grow as they move from the centre and get closer to the player.

Each asteroid clone is removed when it reaches the edge of the STAGE.

11 Run the game again. The stars will move as before, but now you should also see asteroids. The asteroids should have different speeds and sizes. They're going to make it very tricky to pilot a ship through this sector of space!

You're not actually going INTO an asteroid field?!

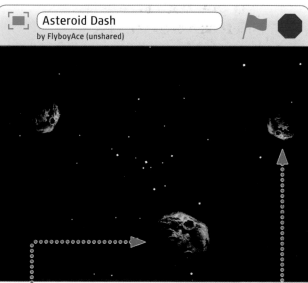

Asteroid Dash
by FlyboyAce (unshared)

The asteroids grow in size as they emerge from the centre, giving the scene a 3D effect.

The smallest asteroids move the fastest.

Add your spaceship

Now you have an asteroid field in your game, it's time to add a space freighter for your player to pilot fearlessly through it.

 12 Click on the paintbrush icon [/] in the NEW SPRITE menu to draw your ship (see pages 14 to 15). Name it "Spaceship". You can use a Scratch sprite to get the game running, then draw a costume later. Centre the ship.

New sprite

Spaceship

Size: Approx. 90 x 90 pixels

Purpose: This is the player's sprite. Its aim is to avoid obstacles and fly for as long as possible.

Fix the hyperdrive

The Star sprite will be coded to make the stars leave trails when your ship uses the hyperdrive. This code activates the hyperdrive effect when the up arrow key is pressed.

 13 Select the Spaceship sprite, then click on the SCRIPTS tab and build the script below.

This is how long the hyperdrive lasts.

Load the "space ripple" sound from the library.

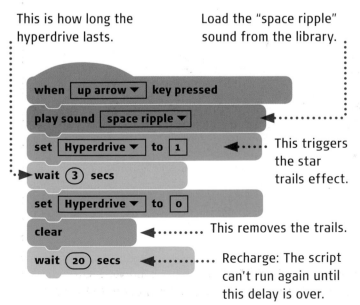

```
when  up arrow ▼  key pressed
play sound  space ripple ▼
set  Hyperdrive ▼  to  1
wait  3  secs
set  Hyperdrive ▼  to  0
clear
wait  20  secs
```

This triggers the star trails effect.

This removes the trails.

Recharge: The script can't run again until this delay is over.

 14 Now run the project. Press the up arrow key to trigger the hyperdrive. A sound will play and each star will leave a trail for a few seconds. The hyperdrive will take 20 seconds to recharge before it can work again.

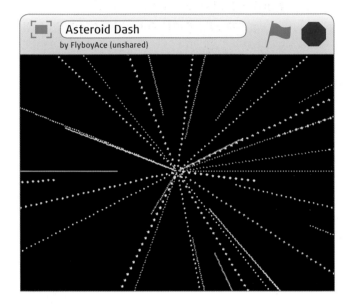

Asteroid Dash
by FlyboyAce (unshared)

Take control!

Now make the code to control your ship. It has a block to keep track of how many parsecs you've flown, which will be your score.

 15 Create a new a variable called "Parsecs" for all sprites, then click "OK". Make sure its box is ticked. Move the variable's window (the parsec meter) to the top left of the STAGE, so it doesn't interfere with the game play.

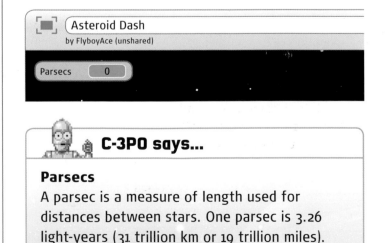

Asteroid Dash
by FlyboyAce (unshared)

Parsecs   0

C-3PO says...

Parsecs

A parsec is a measure of length used for distances between stars. One parsec is 3.26 light-years (31 trillion km or 19 trillion miles).

16 Select the Spaceship sprite and add this new script to set up and control the spaceship. The FOREVER loop around the code takes things back to the start of the game whenever the ship hits an asteroid. Once you've added all the blocks, double-check that they're in the right order and read them through to see if you can figure out what's going on. Take care that the correct blocks are inside the loops and the IF-THEN blocks.

The name here might be different if you're using a Scratch sprite.

The FOREVER loop puts the ship back to its starting position each time it hits an asteroid.

These six blocks set up the spaceship at the start of the game.

This block sets the score (the number of parsecs) to zero at the start of each game.

The blocks inside the REPEAT UNTIL loop control the ship until it's destroyed.

Make sure the IF-THEN blocks that control the ship are inside the REPEAT UNTIL loop, not after it.

You'll need to load the "high hat" sound from the library. Note that the two sound blocks we use here aren't the UNTIL DONE type.

Make sure the value here is −10, not 10.

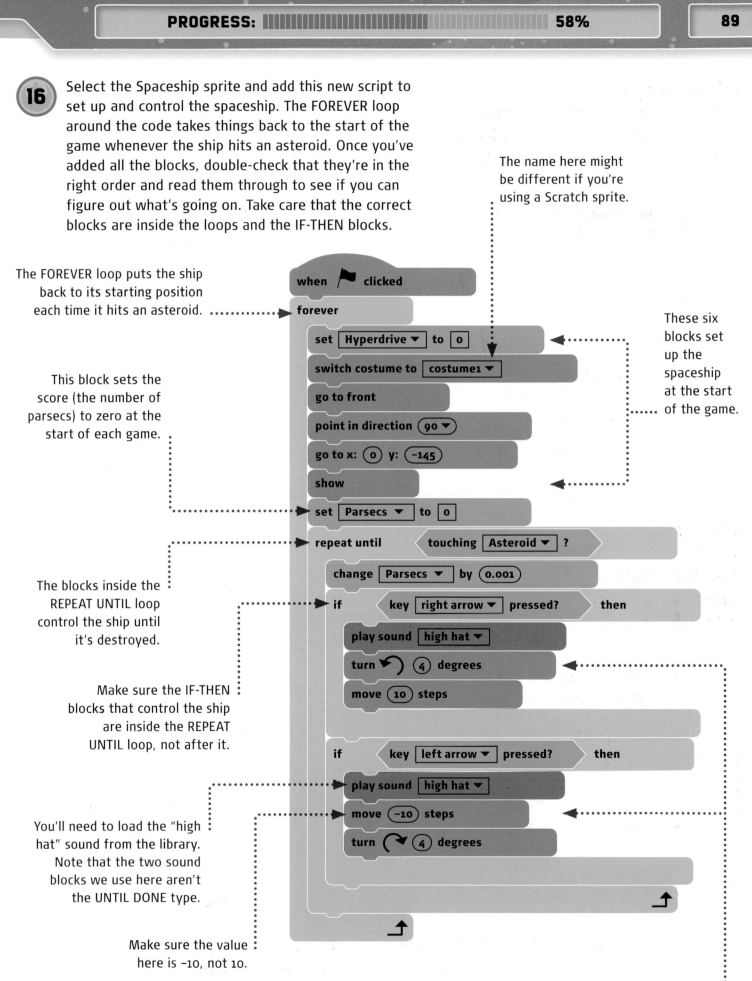

```
when  🏴  clicked
forever
    set  Hyperdrive ▼  to  0
    switch costume to  costume1 ▼
    go to front
    point in direction  90 ▼
    go to x:  0  y:  −145
    show
    set  Parsecs ▼  to  0
    repeat until        touching  Asteroid ▼  ?
        change  Parsecs ▼  by  0.001
        if          key  right arrow ▼  pressed?        then
            play sound  high hat ▼
            turn ↺  4  degrees
            move  10  steps

        if          key  left arrow ▼  pressed?        then
            play sound  high hat ▼
            move  −10  steps
            turn ↻  4  degrees
```

The order of the MOVE and TURN blocks is important. Check that they're in the correct order in both the IF-THEN blocks.

17 Run the game again. Your ship should go around in a circle as you press the left and right arrow keys. If you hit an asteroid, the ship will move back to its starting position for another try and the parsecs score will reset. If it's not working, go back a step and check everything carefully.

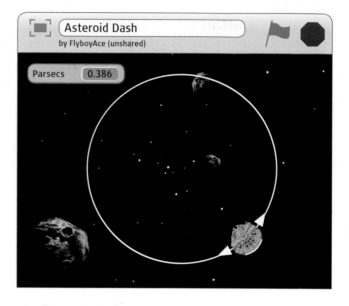

Kabooom!

You don't get away with hitting a fast-moving asteroid without sustaining some damage to your spaceship. Create a spectacular explosion to let the player know it's "Game over!"

18 Select the spaceship in the SPRITES LIST. Open the COSTUMES tab and click on the paintbrush icon [/] to draw an explosion for when the ship hits an obstacle. Note that this is a new costume for the ship, not a new sprite. Make sure it is centred (see page 15).

Click here to create a new costume for the spaceship.

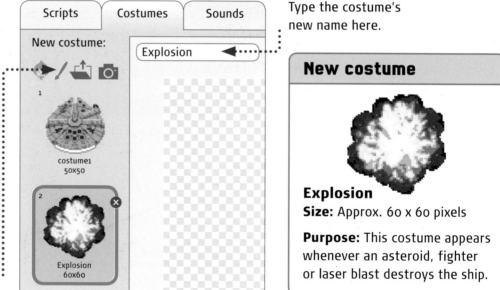

Type the costume's new name here.

New costume

Explosion
Size: Approx. 60 x 60 pixels

Purpose: This costume appears whenever an asteroid, fighter or laser blast destroys the ship.

19 To make an explosion when the spaceship is hit, click on the SCRIPTS tab and add these five blocks to the ship's main script, just inside the end of the FOREVER loop. The explosion will show for a second and then, after three seconds, the game will restart.

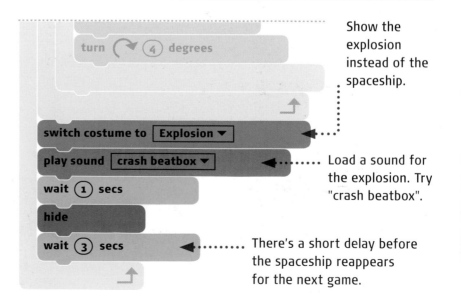

Show the explosion instead of the spaceship.

Load a sound for the explosion. Try "crash beatbox".

There's a short delay before the spaceship reappears for the next game.

20 Run the project again. You should now see and hear an explosion when the spaceship strikes an asteroid.

Enemy attack!

The Empire isn't going to let Han Solo and Chewbacca escape that easily — it'll soon be sending TIE fighters after them. You can create an enemy fighter for your game too by following these steps.

New sprite

Enemy

Size: Approx. 50 x 50 pixels

Purpose: These ships appear at random and fire at the player's ship.

21 To draw the Enemy sprite, click on the paintbrush icon [/] in the NEW SPRITE menu, above the SPRITES LIST. Name your new sprite "Enemy". You can draw a simple shape to get the game working, and then draw a more detailed costume later. Make sure your sprite is centred.

The enemy fighter is rarer than the asteroids: It appears with a 1 in 250 chance each time this loop repeats.

22 Click on the Enemy sprite in the SPRITES LIST. Then click the SCRIPTS tab and add this script to make the ship spiral around the screen. You'll need to create a new variable called "tfSpeed" for this sprite only. Make sure it isn't shown on the STAGE.

Load a sound to use here. Scratch's "motorcycle passing" works well.

Create a message, "Fire!", to trigger the enemy ship's lasers. You'll find the BROADCAST blocks in the brown EVENTS BLOCKS PALETTE.

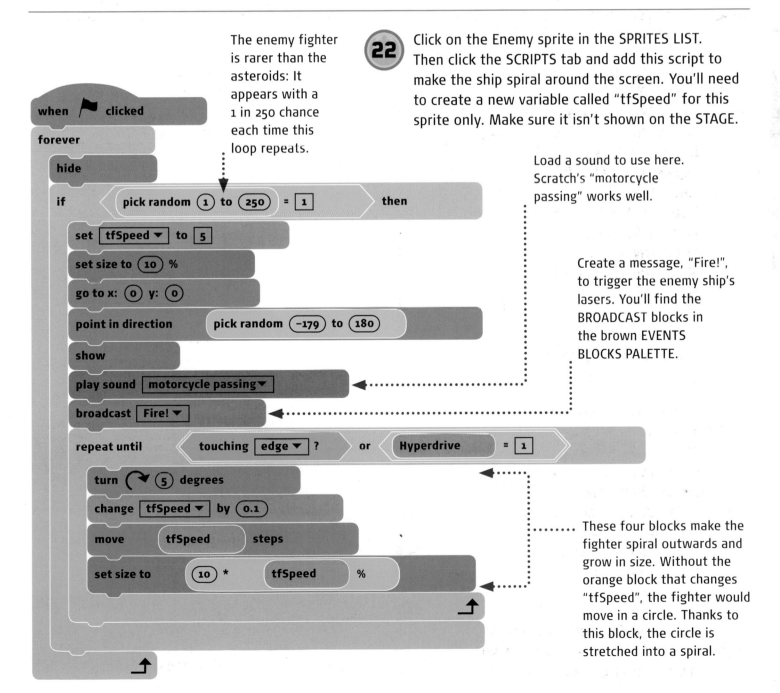

These four blocks make the fighter spiral outwards and grow in size. Without the orange block that changes "tfSpeed", the fighter would move in a circle. Thanks to this block, the circle is stretched into a spiral.

23 Run the game. An enemy fighter should spiral out now and again, but there's no code for it to fire its lasers yet.

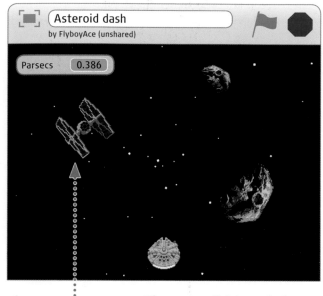

Asteroid dash
by FlyboyAce (unshared)

Parsecs   0.386

.... The enemy fighter spirals out from the centre, appearing to grow larger as it approaches.

24 To draw the Laser Blast sprite, click on the paintbrush icon [/] in the NEW SPRITE menu, above the SPRITES LIST. Name your new sprite "Laser Blast". You can add a simple line to get the game working and add more details later. Make sure your sprite is centred.

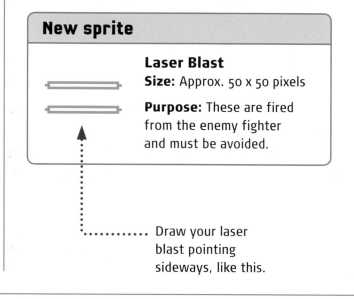

New sprite

Laser Blast
Size: Approx. 50 x 50 pixels

Purpose: These are fired from the enemy fighter and must be avoided.

.... Draw your laser blast pointing sideways, like this.

25 Select the Laser Blast sprite, then click on the SCRIPTS tab and add these scripts. The main script is triggered by the "Fire!" message. Read the script – it should be easy to see how it works. Once you've added this script, run the project and watch the enemy fighter fire at your ship (the laser won't do any damage yet).

when ⚑ clicked
hide

.... The Laser Blast sprite is hidden until it's needed.

.... Note that this initial block isn't the usual WHEN ⚑ CLICKED block.

The laser is aimed at your ship.

It takes a second for the laser to warm up.

The laser blast starts at the enemy fighter.

This block starts the sound effect but the script moves straight on to the next blocks while it plays. Load "laser2" or another sound of your choice.

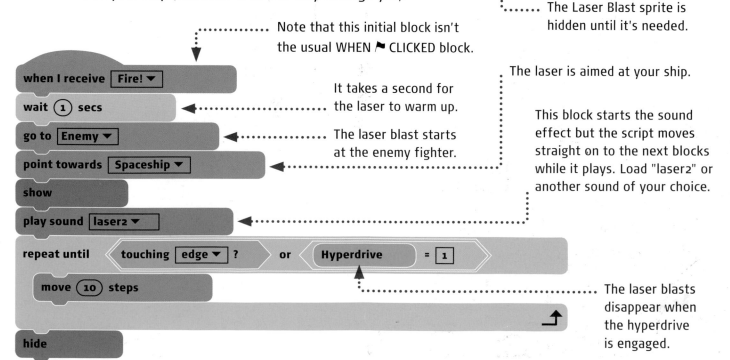

when I receive Fire! ▼
wait 1 secs
go to Enemy ▼
point towards Spaceship ▼
show
play sound laser2 ▼
repeat until ⟨ touching edge ▼ ? ⟩ or ⟨ Hyperdrive = 1 ⟩
    move 10 steps
hide

.... The laser blasts disappear when the hyperdrive is engaged.

26 To make the lasers deadly to your ship, change the "touching Asteroid" test in the spaceship's main script to one that checks for either asteroids or lasers.

Put the TOUCHING ASTEROID block on one side of a green OR block. Then add a new TOUCHING block to the other side of the OR block, and use the drop-down menu to select "Laser Blast".

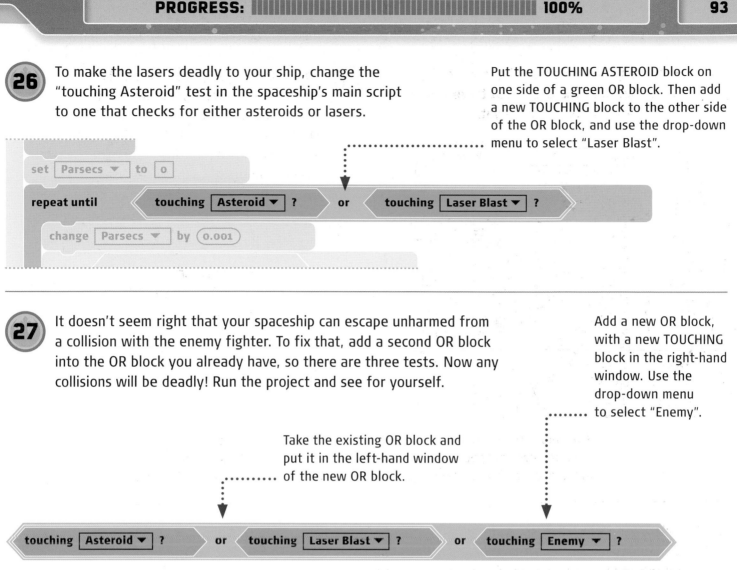

```
set Parsecs ▼ to 0

repeat until    touching Asteroid ▼ ?    or    touching Laser Blast ▼ ?

    change Parsecs ▼ by 0.001
```

27 It doesn't seem right that your spaceship can escape unharmed from a collision with the enemy fighter. To fix that, add a second OR block into the OR block you already have, so there are three tests. Now any collisions will be deadly! Run the project and see for yourself.

Add a new OR block, with a new TOUCHING block in the right-hand window. Use the drop-down menu to select "Enemy".

Take the existing OR block and put it in the left-hand window of the new OR block.

touching Asteroid ▼ ?   or   touching Laser Blast ▼ ?   or   touching Enemy ▼ ?

28 Run the game to check that the asteroids and lasers destroy your ship. Challenge your friends to see who can travel the most parsecs! Also think about what improvements you can make to the game.

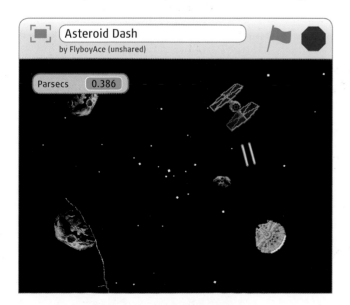

The possibility of successfully navigating an asteroid field is approximately 3,720 to 1.

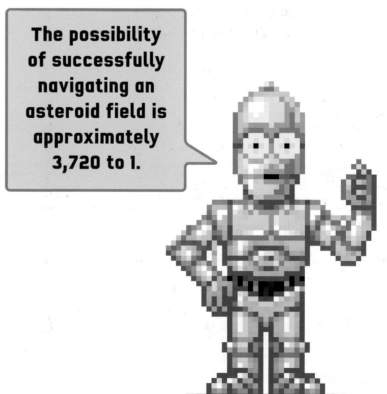

Glossary

algorithm
A set of step-by-step instructions that perform a task. Computer programs are based on algorithms.

animation
Changing pictures quickly to create the illusion of movement.

backdrop
The picture behind the sprites on the STAGE in Scratch.

BACKPACK
A storage area in Scratch that allows you to copy things between projects.

bitmap graphics
Computer drawings stored as a grid of pixels. Compare with *vector graphics*.

block
An instruction in Scratch that can be joined to other blocks to build a script.

branch
A point in a program where two different options are available, such as the IF-THEN-ELSE block.

bug
A coding error that makes a program behave in an unexpected way.

clone
A fully functioning copy of a sprite that can move and run scripts on its own, separate from the original sprite.

collision detection
Programming that detects when two objects in a game are touching.

condition
A "true or false" statement used to make a decision in a program.

coordinates
A pair of numbers that pinpoint an exact spot on the STAGE. Usually written as (x, y).

costume
The picture a sprite shows on the STAGE. Rapidly changing a sprite's costume can create an animation.

data
Information, such as text, symbols or numbers.

debug
To look for and correct errors in a program.

ellipse
An oval

event
Something a computer program can react to, such as a key being pressed or the mouse being clicked.

export
To send something to the computer from Scratch, such as a sprite or a project saved as a computer file.

file
A collection of data stored with a name.

function
Code that carries out a specific task, working like a program within a program. Also called a procedure, subprogram or subroutine.

game physics
Programming to create forces and collisions between objects in a game.

global variable
A variable that can be changed and used by any sprite in a project.

gradient (colour)
A smooth transition from one colour to another, as seen in the sky during a beautiful sunset.

graphics
Visual elements on a screen that are not text, such as pictures, icons and symbols.

GUI
The GUI, or graphical user interface, is the name for the buttons and windows that make up the part of the program you can see and interact with.

hack
An ingenious change to code that makes it do something new or simplifies it. (Also, to access a computer without permission.)

header block
A Scratch block that starts a script, such as the WHEN ⚑ CLICKED block. Also known as a "hat block".

import
To bring something in from outside Scratch, such as a picture or sound clip from the computer's files.

input
Data that is entered into a computer. Keyboards, mice and microphones can be used to input data.

integer
A whole number. An integer does not contain a decimal point and is not written as a fraction.

interface
See GUI

library
A collection of sprites, costumes or sounds that can be used in Scratch programs.

list
A collection of items stored in a numbered order.

local variable
A variable that can be changed by only one sprite. Each copy or clone of a sprite has its own separate version of the variable.

loop
A part of a program that repeats itself, removing the need to type out the same piece of code multiple times.

memory
A computer chip inside a computer that stores data.

message
A way to send information between sprites.

network
A group of interconnected computers that exchange data. The internet is a giant network.

operating system (OS)
The program that controls everything on a computer, such as Windows, OS X or Linux.

operator
A Scratch block that uses data to work something out, such as checking whether two values are equal or adding two numbers together.

physics
The science of how things move and affect each other. Physics is often important in simulations and

games – for example, to create realistic gravity.

pixel art
A drawing made of giant pixels or blocks, mimicking the appearance of graphics in early computer games.

pixels
The coloured dots on a screen that make up graphics.

program
A set of instructions that a computer follows in order to complete a task.

programming language
A language that is used to give instructions to a computer.

project
Scratch's name for a program and all the sprites, sounds and backdrops that go with it.

random
A function in a computer program that allows unpredictable outcomes. Useful when creating games.

run
The command to make a program start.

script
A stack of instruction blocks under a header block that are run in order.

software
Programs that run on a computer and control how it works.

sprite
A picture on the STAGE in Scratch that a script can move and change.

STAGE
The screen-like area of the Scratch interface in which projects run.

statement
The smallest complete instruction a programming language can be broken down into.

tweak
A small change made to something to make it work better or differently.

variable
A place to store data that can change in a program, such as the player's score. A variable has a name and a value.

vector graphics
Computer drawings stored as collections of shapes, making them easier to change. Compare with *bitmap graphics*.

> We'll see each other again. I believe that.

Dr Jon Woodcock MA (OXON)

Jon has a degree in physics from the University of Oxford and a PhD in computational astrophysics from the University of London. He started coding at the age of eight and has programmed all kinds of computers, from single-chip microcontrollers to world-class supercomputers. His many projects include giant space simulations, research in high-tech companies and intelligent robots made from junk. Jon has a passion for science and technology education, giving talks on space and running computer programming clubs in schools. He has worked on numerous science and technology books, including DK's *Computer Coding Games for Kids*, *Computer Coding Projects for Kids* and DK's series of coding workbooks.

Scratch

Scratch is a programming language and online community where you can create your own interactive stories, games and animations – and share your creations with others around the world. In the process of designing and programming Scratch projects, young people learn to think creatively, reason systematically and work collaboratively. Scratch is a project of the Lifelong Kindergarten group at the MIT Media Lab. It is available for free at: **scratch.mit.edu.**

Acknowledgements

DK would like to thank Jon Hall for his artwork; Kiki Prottsman for the foreword; Steve Setford and Peter Radcliffe for their editorial and design work; Natalie Edwards, Katy Lennon, Sarah Rinzler and Anni Sander for editorial assistance; Anne Sharples for design assistance and Julia March for proofreading. The publisher would also like to thank Brett Rector, Michael Siglain, Christine Talarides and Leland Chee at Lucasfilm; Chelsea Alon at Disney and the MIT Media Lab for creating Scratch.

How to get Scratch

If your computer is always connected to the internet, it's best to run Scratch online. If not, you need to download and install the offline version.

Scratch 2.0

It's important to use Scratch 2.0 with this book because the projects won't work with the older version (Scratch 1.4). To check which version you have, see if the STAGE is on the right of your Scratch screen. If it is, then you have version 1.4.

Online

▶ Visit the Scratch website at: **scratch.mit.edu** and click on "Join Scratch" to create an account with a username and password. You'll need an email address, too.

▶ Online Scratch runs in your web browser, so go to the website and click on "Create" at the top of the screen. The Scratch interface will open.

▶ You don't have to save your work, since the online version of Scratch saves projects automatically.

▶ As long as you have a recent web browser, online Scratch should work on Windows, Mac and Linux computers. This includes the latest Raspberry Pi, but the games may run slowly.

Offline

▶ Visit the Scratch website at: **scratch.mit.edu/ scratch2download** and follow the instructions to download and install Scratch on your computer.

▶ Scratch will appear as an icon on your desktop, just like any other installed program. Double-click on the Scratch Cat icon to get going.

▶ You'll need to save your project by clicking on the File menu and selecting "Save". Scratch will ask you where to save your work – check with the computer's owner.

▶ Offline Scratch works well on Windows and Mac computers, but often runs into trouble on Linux computers.